To Gail, my wife for 55 years. Since the first day we met,
she has continuously demonstrated the power of generosity to me.
The spirit of Jesus is in her.

To Patty, whose full-life generosity attracted me from the moment
I met her and who has, through her modeling, infused it into
our children and our marriage for the last 25+ years.

We both thank you for allowing us to tell the story
of your influence on us in this small way.

INTRODUCTION
(Gordon MacDonald)

ONE DECEMBER DAY, MARK (MY SON) AND I MET AT THE LOCAL STARBUCKS for coffee. Soon our conversation turned to the topic of generosity.

Generosity? Why generosity?

The previous night we'd gone with our wives to see a musical production of Charles Dickens' *A Christmas Carol*. During the evening, the story of Ebenezer Scrooge's journey from scoundrel to saint had captured our attention in a fresh new way.

We recalled the early scenes when Scrooge made his first appearance on stage. He was hateful, the embodiment of mean-spiritedness and greed. He had a toxic effect on everyone who crossed his path. No wonder people did everything they could to avoid him. Even the stray dogs on the street hid in the alleys when they saw him coming.

While Ebenezer Scrooge's story centers around his obsession with money, it did not escape us that Scrooge was equally boorish in every other aspect of his life. He had no friends, no community or church to which he was loyal, no charitable interests, and certainly no evidence of admirable character. Businesswise, his treatment of both his clients and his one employee was deplorable.

In short, there was nothing good to say about the Ebenezer Scrooge we met at the beginning of Dickens' *A Christmas Carol*. The man, we agreed, was a monster.

Most people with a Christian point of view would agree that Scrooge needed one thing more than anything else: a *splendid transformation*, which would have to begin at the core of his being and radiate outward until it touched everything about his character and personality.

Over the course of our evening at the theater, that's exactly what happened. The formerly toxic Ebenezer Scrooge became splendidly transformed. We coined the term BeScrooged to describe what happened to him.

As the evening at the theater neared its end, those whom Ebenezer had formerly despised—both family and friends—became his loved ones. The once run-down neighborhood where he lived changed into a cheerful place. The company culture at Scrooge and Marley was dramatically altered. In short, wherever the BeScrooged Ebenezer went, everything was transformed.

As we rehearsed the story of Ebenezer Scrooge the next morning, we found ourselves using the term *full-life generosity* to describe the man he became.

Full-life. The story was not just about his changed attitude toward money. It was about his whole being: his character, his personality, and his fresh love for people, especially the weak and struggling.

As he fell into the habit of giving, his efforts always exceeded anyone's expectations. He loved to give. And that meant he held nothing back. That's generosity.

We think that Jesus had *full-life generosity* in mind when he said, "*It is more blessed to give than to receive.*"

As Mark and I talked on, we acknowledged to one another that the new Scrooge at the end of Dickens' story inspired us to examine ourselves and to determine the distances we had to go before we could feel confident that we were fully generous men. Was there a possibility, we asked, that all of us are in constant need of BeScroogement?

That December conversation over coffee laid the tracks for this book.

TAKER TO FULL-LIFE GIVER

Consider the reading of this book to be a brief spiritual journey. We will offer you the opportunity to reflect on your own pattern of generosity. In an upcoming lesson, you will find something we call Ebenezer's Ladder. It describes several ascending categories of generosity patterns. It is likely that you will find yourself on a particular rung of the ladder, and the question will occur: What would it take to climb a rung or two higher?

These rungs and their descriptions are not meant to embarrass you, but merely to help you explore your own attitudes toward full-life generosity. For those who sincerely wish to grow in full-life effectiveness, this is a chance to determine where you are and where you need to go.

Full-Life Generosity?

Full-life generous people find their inspiration in the Bible and from future generations of Christ followers.

- They see *full-life generosity* at the core of the character of God.
- *They see full-life generosity in the leadership of Moses when he taught the Israelites how to bring the "first fruits" of their work to the altar.*
- *They see full-life generosity everywhere in the life of Jesus: his investment in the lives of the disciples, his engagement with those who were routinely ignored (children, the poor, the diseased, the ostracized), and his graciousness to his enemies.*
- *They see full-life generosity in the work of the Holy Spirit ,who equips and empowers people to shower the earth with the gift of God's salvation.*
- *They see full-life generosity in the twelve apostles the Lord trained to be selfless, redemptive, and sacrificial in their lives and sent out to cover the earth with his gospel.*
- *They see full-life generosity in the lives of the first generation of Christ-followers who founded a dynamic community of vigorously caring people throughout the Ancient Near East.*

- *And, finally, they see full-life generosity in the efforts of the first Christians, who expressed their faith by serving the poor, visiting the sick, looking out for the widow and orphan, embracing the homeless, and proclaiming the saving love of Jesus to the spiritually lost.*

Taking these inspirational principles into account is why we have defined Full-Life Generosity in the following way:

Choosing one day at a time to live generously, as Jesus did, in all that we think, we are and we do.

Generous people are Selfless: they put the interests of others before themselves;

Generous people are Redemptive: they extend God-given grace and healing to a broken world;

Generous people are Sacrificial: they give abundantly as the Holy Spirit reveals the Kingdom opportunities around them;

Generous people are "all-in:" they commit their skills, their spiritual strengths, their influence and their assets for the cause of Christ and His Kingdom.

Today there are full-life generous people all around us that have decided each day when they wake up each morning and put their feet on the ground they are going to live a different day—a full life of generosity. Some examples?

- *A man who's taken early retirement and volunteered to work forty hours a week on behalf of homeless people.*
- *A woman who possesses a remarkable ability to encourage people. Wherever she goes, people are lifted and inspired to grow and serve.*
- *The executive that realizes that they need to serve their team by representing being selfless, redemptive and sacrificial to his employees.*
- *A man who says, "I'm happiest when I play the number two role, the servant role, and make other people shine in the pursuit of things they need to accomplish."*
- *A woman who loves children. She welcomes them to her backyard, tells them stories, teaches them songs, and introduces them to Jesus.*
- *A husband and wife who have developed a financial plan that maximizes their ability to support a community project in a developing nation.*
- *A small group of men and women who raise money to drill clean water wells for villages in Central American countries.*
- *A bus driver who starts every day declaring his intention to show the love of God to each passenger on his bus.*
- *Children who earn money to support a village development program in Central Africa.*
- *Teenagers who volunteer to tutor small children in a reading initiative.*

- *An older woman who walks around her community retrieving coins that people have lost or left behind and sending them to an organization that serves the poor.*

These examples demonstrate the variety of ways that people can live out the concept of full-life generosity.

It's All About Grace

The word *generous* matches up easily with the word grace. In fact, the two words come close to being synonymous. They both could be said to represent a thoroughly Christian idea: *the practice of giving without concern for anything in return.*

Here is St. Paul speaking to the Corinthian church about full-life generosity, or the grace of Christ:

> *"You know the grace [the generosity] of our Lord Jesus Christ, that though he was rich, yet for your sake he became poor, that you through his poverty might become rich." (2 Corinthians 8:9)*

When Paul wrote this, he was challenging the relatively affluent Corinthians to face up to their lack of *generosity*. What better way to do that than to remind them that Jesus was the supreme model of full-life generosity? If he was generous to that extent, could the Corinthians, who called themselves Christ-followers, settle for anything less? Can any of us?

WEEK ONE

MANY WORDS COMMUNICATE THE ABSOLUTE OPPOSITE OF FULL-LIFE GENEROSITY. One of them is greed. Other words might be selfish, cheapskate, unkind, stingy, miser, cruel, and merciless. Most of us associate these words with someone who thinks only of himself, his status in life, and his possessions.

In this first week, we'll look at seven biblical examples of these sorts of non-generous characteristics. These stories are certainly not very cheerful, but they serve as a reminder that all of us need every once in a while. A life which is devoid of full-life generosity is, in God's eyes, a life wasted.

First, a few words from Mr. Ebenezer Scrooge, who will unfold the story of his BeScroogement in four segments. As he walks us through some very special moments in his life (most of us are well-acquainted with them), we should consider what he can teach us.

In rehearsing Ebenezer's story, we've found it necessary to abbreviate aspects of Charles Dickens' amazing work, *A Christmas Carol*. And we've taken liberties with the beautiful 19th-century English language and literary style that Dickens employed. We've even dared to add a few imaginative alterations to his story. Students of English literature will doubtless shudder at what we've done. But we mean no harm.

In the next seven days you will become acquainted with seven "Scrooges" in the Bible. Each one is filled with a spirit of selfishness and greed. Think through their lives: the "idols" they worshipped, the choices they made, the opportunities they squandered, the people they hurt. You might want to ask yourself—as we did—*to what extent is there any of this spirit in me?*

1

"When I think back to those spiritually empty days I see clearly that I had reached a point where I offered nothing beneficial to anyone in the world around me."

Meet Ebenezer Scrooge

My name is Scrooge, Ebenezer Scrooge. I'm an investment guy who's been around (book-wise, anyway) for almost 175 years, thanks to one of England's greatest authors, Charles Dickens.

Many would say—and justifiably so—that I made my debut as one of the meanest, most selfish men in all of English literature. My "creator," Mr. Dickens, described me as "a *squeezing, wrenching, grasping, scraping, clutching, covetous old sinner.*" Words like these leave little to the imagination as to the kind of man I used to be.

Ask anyone who knew me in those days, and they will tell you that I worshiped an "idol" called *money.* This monetary obsession of mine had nothing to do with wanting to buy things (I've never liked spending) or gaining a place on the list of the world's richest people. And I certainly wasn't motivated to make money so I could give it to some college or church or community project (I was hardly a major donor).

No, my idolization of money was all about one thing that could be reduced to the form of a mission statement: Accumulate enough wealth so that I will never need anybody. But how much is "enough" when you want to avoid needing anybody?

When I think back to those spiritually empty days, I see clearly that I had reached a point where I offered nothing beneficial to anyone in the world around me. No one ever heard an encouraging word come from my mouth. No one was ever invited to my home as a guest. If I'd had friends, I never would have extended a helping hand. I was merciless, vindictive, and unforgiving toward people who crossed me. I was insensitive to the sufferings of others. I hadn't the slightest interest in being part of a circle of caring friends. Therefore, it shouldn't surprise you if I also acknowledge that my reputation for financial generosity was virtually nonexistent.

Today, I am a totally different man, thanks to an unforgettable set of experiences I had one Christmas many years ago. In the space of just a few hours, everything in my life changed. Gone was that spirit of *selfishness.* In its place came a new spirit, the spirit of *generosity... full-life generosity.* I call this experience BeScroogement, or becoming *BeScrooged.*

Three Miserable Encounters: My Nephew, Fred

BeScroogement began for me on a Christmas Eve afternoon when my nephew, Fred, burst through the front door of my company, Scrooge and Marley, bellowing "Merry Christmas." Over and over: "Merry Christmas, Merry Christmas!"

Fred did this sort of thing every Christmas Eve, and I just hated it. But Fred's exuberance could never be stopped.

What made it worse this time was that my clerk, Bob Cratchit, went crazy when Fred arrived. The two of them laughed and danced and sang like children. Then they began to chat about their families and what they'd bought their children for Christmas. Their conversation got louder and louder until I exploded. I shouted at them to shut up.

"How," I yelled, "can anyone concentrate on business when you insist on carrying on like this?"

Fred was not to be muzzled by my temper tantrum. He yelled back at me, "God save you, Uncle." Then he started toward me with the intention of hugging me. Hugging me, mind you! I tried pushing him off, but Fred was a stronger man than I realized. He was going to hug me whether I liked it or not.

Finally, they quieted down, and Fred had the temerity to invite me to come to his home for dinner on Christmas afternoon. He wanted me, he said, to be a part of a joyful family for the day.

"Humbug!" I shouted. "What do you have to be joyful about? You're as poor as they come."

Fred didn't react to my crassness. Instead, he said, "Uncle, Christmas is a great time for loving people, forgiving them, and treating everyone with dignity. Christmas doesn't make anyone rich as far as I know. But it is very good for one's soul."

These words were typical of Fred. I'll say now what I would never have said then: Fred has always been the epitome of *full-life generosity*. He invites people like me to his home. He's good at coming alongside discouraged people. And he's always nearby when his neighbors have a need. He must know every person in his neighborhood ... by name. That's the kind of big-hearted man Fred has always been.

You know, I suspect Fred always anticipated this Christmas-Eve banter between us with a fiendish kind of joy. And I think Fred really believed that the day would come when my reaction to his annual Christmas invitation would be different—that I would actually join the family and participate in their happiness.

Finally, after a few more hugs and dances with Bob Cratchit, Fred left the office. But not before he had me in a sweat, my body trembling, my breath coming in short bursts. Take it from one who knows: a man with a greedy, Scrooge-like spirit cannot stand the presence of a man who insists on being generous.

Three Miserable Encounters: My Clerk, Bob Cratchit

With Fred gone Bob Cratchit and I returned to our work.

In those days Cratchit, his wife, and their several children lived well below the poverty level. If truth be told, everything about their lives was hardship. By contrast, I took home forty (maybe sixty) times what I paid Bob. Today I'm embarrassed that, as his employer, I never appreciated the inequities in this arrangement.

One of the Cratchit children was a dearly loved but seriously ill boy, Tim. No one thought he would live a long life. If Bob and his wife had been in a better financial condition, things might have been different. But the kind of medical attention the kid needed was not affordable for people as disadvantaged as the Cratchits.

I confess that it never crossed my mind that some financial assistance from me could have redirected the course of Tim Cratchit's life. Here was his father working beside me every day, and I never once thought to ask, "How's Timmy doing?" or "Is there anything I could do to make things easier for you?" My soul—if I had one—simply didn't work that way.

Late in the afternoon, a heated exchange erupted between Bob Cratchit and me when he asked if he could have Christmas Day off. I planned to be at my desk on Christmas Day, so why shouldn't he be at his also? "Christmas keeps men from doing business," I yelled.

A few minutes later, when I'd calmed down, I muttered in a most patronizing way, "Cratchit, it seems to me that Christmas is just an excuse for getting something for free. But if you must have a whole day off, take it." And then, so I would have last word, I added, "Make sure you're here even earlier on the following day."

How can anyone live with or work for a man such as I used to be? And how do you sleep at night if you *are* the man I once was? Remembering my vicious (and that's what it was) treatment of Bob Cratchit in those days makes me want to crawl in a hole. BeScroogement, I was to learn, was the only hope for me. I needed a change of life that began at soul-level and rose to touch every part of me.

Three Miserable Encounters: Two Charitable Men

Toward the end of that Christmas Eve afternoon, two men entered the office asking for a corporate donation on behalf of the poor in our neighborhood.

"We would like to collect funds to do something nice at Christmas for those who are poor and suffering," one of them said.

My response? Today, I can hardly believe I actually said these words. "There are prisons and workhouses for people who have nothing," I said. "Send them there."

When I said this, one of the men tried to reason with me. "Many people would rather die than go to a workhouse."

My response? "If they would rather die, then let them go ahead. It will lower the surplus population."

When the two men expressed disbelief at my words, I cut them off and shouted angrily, "Why don't you just leave me alone?"

It wouldn't be long before I would hear these words quoted back to me.

Well, if you think about the way I handled my nephew Fred, intimidated my clerk, Bob Cratchit, and blew off the two men who asked me for a gift for the poor, you begin to understand what a mean old miser I was capable of being.

So, what happens to a man like me if there is no change, no BeScroogement? What happens when the time comes for him to leave this world and pass into eternity? More importantly, how does God deal with people who are blessed with various forms of "wealth" but who fail to use them responsibly and generously?

Pause and Reflect

What are some of the methods Scrooge used to disguise his empty heart? What are some of the qualities in the people who surrounded Scrooge that hint of full-life generosity?

When that Christmas Eve ended, I had no idea what I was about to experience. I could not have imagined that, in a few hours, I would begin a soul-wrenching process that usually takes a lifetime to complete. But somewhere—in heaven, maybe—a decision had been made. In the space of just one night, Ebenezer Scrooge—like it or not—would have his life turned inside out. And when that night turned into day, he would be a new man.

BeScroogement was underway.

DAY 1:
CHOICES

READ GENESIS 13, GENESIS 19

"Abram lived in the land of Canaan while Lot lived among the cities of the plain and pitched his tents near Sodom." (Genesis 13:2)

LOT! HE WAS A CLEVER YOUNG MAN, THIS NEPHEW OF THE GREAT PATRIARCH, Abraham. Wherever the uncle went, Lot followed, listening, learning, and imitating. He was always on the lookout for personal advantage.

We might call the two men business partners, but it's clear Abraham was the senior. As he prospered, Lot did also. In other words, Abraham's rising tide lifted Lot's boat.

But maybe their partnership was limited to business. You may wonder if Lot also shared Abraham's journey toward faith in God. This doesn't appear to be the case.

There came a day when the business arrangement began to unravel. The uncle/nephew enterprise began to outgrow the territory. Frequent disputes (probably over water rights and lush pastures) between Abraham's and Lot's herdsmen became a serious problem. The fact that there were hostile people living in the area didn't help.

The solution was a parting of the ways. They chose to dissolve the partnership and make space between the two working groups.

The custom in such situations called for the senior partner, in this case Abraham, to exercise the right of first choice in terms of land. For unexplained reasons, Abraham relinquished that right and offered Lot the chance to choose first. This meant that wherever Lot chose to go, Abraham was content to head in the opposite direction.

Was this gesture evidence of an older man getting soft, or was it evidence that Abraham was learning to live by faith? Was it his way of saying that he was putting his business, his security, and his wealth in the hands of God?

Lot, the more devious of the two, made his decision quickly. Perhaps he was concerned that Abraham might change his mind.

His choice was based on what *seemed* the best for his flocks and herds. The verdant plains of the Jordan valley—irrigated, filled with the promise of prosperity—seemed a pretty good deal to him. Lot also had to be aware of the intriguing city of Sodom.

Given Lot's choice, Abraham headed for the hilly country, seemingly less productive, but (but!) ...marked somehow with the favor of God and the promise of a great future family line.

You could say that Lot opted for whatever increased his wealth. Abraham, on the other hand, set his sights on the long-range expectation of a family line that came with the blessing of God. The result? Over the course of his life, Abraham became a fully generous person.

Lot's end-game was a pitiable one. He and his family were soon mesmerized by the seductions of Sodom, a city long associated with moral lawlessness of every kind. A beautiful place, perhaps, but a culture that was dangerous to the soul. Sodom was hardly a place to bring up a family or to establish a durable legacy.

It is not surprising that, before long, everything in Lot's life collapsed. Everything! Home, family, assets—gone! When Lot exited Sodom, rescued only by the grace of God and Abraham's power, life as he knew it came to an end. He ended up a broken man.

Lot's story should inspire us to examine ourselves. One way to start is to *think lots about Lot*—the bright young man who lived on selfish values and purposes but never cultivated his soul. As a result, when the moment came for him to make strategic decisions about his future, his family, and his work, everything imploded. Greed-oriented decision-making has that effect.

Would Lot have listened to Scrooge if they'd had a chance to talk? Can you imagine Ebenezer saying to Lot, "Before you make a business decision, young man, you should not only count the cost in terms of profits, but also in terms of how your choices will affect your soul...and the souls of those you say you love the most."

Ebenezer asks: What are the earliest hints that Lot might be headed for disaster? What details show the kind of man Abraham was becoming?

Reflection: Have you ever made a choice that had unintended negative consequences? What led you to make that choice?

BeScrooged Activity: Prayer: Ask God to speak and show you during these next few weeks how you might see your life through a new lens--the lens of full-life generosity.

DAY 2:
OBSESSION

READ I KINGS 21

"Ahab lay on his bed sulking and refused to eat...His wife, Jezebel, came in and asked him, 'Why are you so sullen. Why won't you eat?'" (I Kings 21:4-5)

HE WAS AN INCREDIBLY WEAK MAN, THIS KING OF ISRAEL NAMED AHAB. He was delusional if he thought he possessed real power. Had he been more perceptive, he would have realized he was little more than a figurehead, while off in the shadows a collection of pagan priests controlled the country. Their power was derived from the patronage of Ahab's wife, Jezebel, one of the most hateful people in the Bible.

Among the biblical accounts of Ahab's life, there is a short but significant story that tells the reader all he needs to know about the character and conduct of this man. It also serves as a warning about how easy it is for someone, imagining that he has power, to cross a moral line and confiscate things from others simply because he wants them.

A man named Naboth owned a vineyard of some value. The vineyard was located in the shadow of the king's palace, and the king desired it for himself. So he made Naboth an offer that the man wasn't expected to refuse. Ahab suggested that they pull off a land-trade or Naboth sell his vineyard outright.

But Naboth had no interest in either option. The land, he said, had been in the family for too long. No deal.

"So Ahab went home, sullen and angry," the story-teller says. "He lay on his bed and refused to eat." This is a king, mind you, sulking because someone told him "no."

Greed and power can do this to people. Accustomed to hearing "yes," many are in danger of being thrown off balance when someone actually says "no."

Enter the cunning Jezebel, who should have told Ahab to grow up, but didn't. Rather, she sized up the situation and took the action that Ahab probably wanted to take but lost the nerve. She arranged for Naboth's murder—by stoning.

When the word came back that Naboth was dead, Ahab didn't hesitate to claim the land for himself.

Reading through biblical biographies reveals the extent of human depravity. In Ahab's case, we see clearly how possessions (power, land, money, and precious commodities) can, if unchecked, distort and destroy the soul.

The outcome of Ahab's story shows God's displeasure with greed. While Ahab was preparing to possess Naboth's vineyard, he was confronted by the prophet Elijah, who bluntly informed him that his crime against a comparatively powerless man would ultimately cost him his own life. In the end, Ahab died a slow death on the battlefield.

The majority of us will likely never sink to the "low" that Ahab and Jezebel did. But it is not a bad thing for us to ponder whether we are capable of Ahab- or Jezebel-like behavior.

You may wonder if Scrooge could have helped Ahab to see where his inability to be satisfied was leading him. "Come on, Ahab," one can hear Scrooge say, "it's only a piece of land. Certainly not worth a man's life. Have you become so obsessed with stuff that you have lost your spiritual moorings?"

If left unchecked, Ahab's kind of greed can morph into a dangerous force and cause incalculable damage.

Ebenezer asks: What was the idol in Ahab's life? What strikes you about Ahab's character? What was driving him and his decisions? Where did he leave himself open to failure? What role could Jezebel have played if she had sought to be a fully generous person?

Reflection: Have you ever been in a situation where you became preoccupied with getting something for yourself that you couldn't afford, you didn't deserve, or was harmful to you? What lesson did you learn through the experience?

BeScrooged Activity: Open your eyes and think deeply about any barriers that may be keeping you from an open-heart/open-hand approach to full-life generosity. What may be fogging up your vision?

DAY 3:
DISCONTENTMENT

READ I KINGS 10:14-11:13;
DEUTERONOMY 17:14-20

"King Solomon was greater in riches and wisdom than all the other kings of the earth. The whole world sought audience with Solomon to hear the wisdom God had put in his heart." (I Kings 10:23-24)

SOLOMON WAS BORN INTO ROYALTY AND GIFTED WITH A WISDOM so impressive that the whole world, it is said, came to observe how he governed his people. This man was on a fast track to becoming Israel's greatest king. How brilliant of him to have asked Israel's God for insight that was a mile deep.

Then something went sour in him at soul-level. Was the reason boredom, or a growing obsession with pleasure? There is also the possibility that he became addicted to wealth, and it began to re-shape his core values. And we can't forget his unbridled attraction to the opposite gender. He seems to have collected women like some moguls acquire antique cars.

It almost seems as if there are two different men crowding his life story: one man started out as wise, noble, and judicious, and the other man ended up debauched and infatuated by glamour and power.

You may wonder if Solomon ever read Moses's warning to Israel about the propensity of people in power to crash and burn morally and spiritually. Was he aware that kings should not accumulate many horses, nor hoard huge amounts of silver and gold, nor warehouse many wives with subversive spiritual orientations?

Did anyone remind Solomon that Moses urged future kings to revisit these warnings every day? Apparently Moses—perhaps because he grew up in a palace himself—knew how easy it was for kings to lose their spiritual grounding and think of themselves as superior and unaccountable to the people they ruled.

Eventually, Solomon blew off everything Moses said about the conduct of kings. Then came the moment when God said something like, "That's enough, Solomon! You're done!"

How could Solomon have been so shrewd in the ruling of his kingdom and so stupid when it came to managing himself? Is this the end result when people fail to observe God's law? Is this what happens when one strays from doing things God's way and assumes that no one is ever going to tell him "no"? Is this what greed looks like? Never enough?

Not many of us will ever become as prosperous as Solomon. But a lot of us hear the same seductive inner voice he heard. We hear that we can have it all, do it all, experience it all. And suddenly, like Solomon, we become trapped by our own unchecked obsessions.

I hear Scrooge speaking to Solomon: "Sol, I once fell into a trap not unlike yours. I once had a lovely fiancée, a good job working for a generous boss, and a future with no discernible obstacles. But then I became romanced by the notion that there could (or should) be something more. When I headed out to find it, I discovered to my chagrin that I'd lost all the best things in life. Solomon, listen to me: nothing warps a man like greed. That first half of your life was all about full-life generosity. The second half? There are no words."

Ebenezer asks: When was Solomon at the peak of his wisdom? What were the attractions that eventually weakened him? What happens to us when we can't satisfy our various desires?

Reflection: What would make it possible for you to experience a greater level of contentment in your life? What are the issues that lead you to an experience of discontent?

BeScrooged Activity: What brings you contentment in life? Try to complete this sentence: "I'll be content when (or if) _____."

DAY 4:
DEAD-END DECISIONS

READ LUKE 12:13-21

"The ground of a certain rich man produced a good crop. He thought to himself, 'What shall I do? I have no place to store my crops.'" (Luke 12:8)

ONE DAY JESUS TALKED ABOUT AN AFFLUENT FARMER WHO WAS FACED WITH a life-altering decision. His farm had produced a bumper crop so large that it exceeded all of his storage capacity.

The great question he had to answer was what to do with this super-abundance.

"He thought to himself," the Lord said. In other words, the farmer experienced a moment of strategic choice-making, the choice between suffocating greed and full-life generosity.

In this story the greed option seemed—*seemed*, mind you—to promise a lifetime of security, comfort, and pleasure. Greed said, "Enlarge, hoard, use this extra wealth only for yourself. Oh, and if you can, keep adding more to your net worth."

Although the story never mentions it, there must have been a full-life generosity option. Imagine what that option might look like in modern terms.

A portion of the business surplus could be allocated to rehabilitate a neighborhood. A school could be constructed for the benefit of young people in the community. A research project could be funded that just might neutralize a dreaded disease. A clean water system could be installed in a far-off community where sanitary conditions are abominable. Why couldn't this farmer have given himself to mentoring younger farmers who needed someone to help them get started?

Sadly, as far as we know, the man in Jesus's story never considered the full-life generosity option. He thought only of himself. That was the extent, the shallowness, of his soul-level thinking.

"I will tear down my barns and build bigger ones and there I will store all my grain and my goods. And I'll say to myself, 'You have plenty of good things laid up for many years. Take life easy; eat, drink, and be merry.'" (Luke 12:18)

The man, Jesus said, was a fool.

This is an ancient version of a contemporary story. The story implies that the good life is measured by what one has stored away in the bank. The story promises that nothing can go wrong as long as one's net worth is beyond counting. The story suggests that soul-peace is calculated in terms of what one possesses.

The farmer's story ended with judgment. "But God said to him…" (Luke 12:20) Oh… was God in this story? Yes, of course. Isn't he always?

Conveniently, the farmer had forgotten about divine accountability. If he selfishly used what he had been given, he would have to explain his actions to his Creator.

What can we conclude about this man's foolish view of life? First, that he was unaware of his inner life, or spiritual center, where his financial standing meant nothing. Second, that he was blind to the needs of the larger world, where he could make investments of charity and service that had eternal value. Finally, that he was ignorant of God's presence in his life and what being part of building the kingdom of God offers.

Ebenezer asks: What was the assumption upon which this farmer based his business decisions? What was missing in his plan? What were the implications of his choices for himself and his family?

Reflection: To what extent is this story an extreme example of the way we are tempted to think about our own situations?

BeScrooged Activity: Identify one or two areas in your life where you sense the need to be more intentional. Ask yourself if there are one or two areas of life where you need to scale down your lifestyle..

DAY 5:
RELIGIOUS "SELFISHNESS"

READ II CORINTHIANS 8-9

"Just as you excel in everything—in faith, in speech, in knowledge, in complete earnestness, and in your love for us—see that you also excel in this grace of giving."
II (Corinthians 8:7)

MOST CHURCHES, SEEN FROM THE INSIDE, ARE A BIT MESSY. Few, however, could exceed the disarray among those who populated the church in Corinth. Read St. Paul's two letters to them, and you'll visualize a church that was marked with divisiveness, theological confusion, sex scandals, legal disputes, and destructive hero-worship.

To make matters worse, the "better-off" members of the church tended to treat the struggling members with *disdain*. Compare *disdain* to words like contempt, insensitivity, neglect, or stinginess, and you will begin to understand just how superficial the church in Corinth was becoming.

In fact, the church in Corinth reflected the larger culture of the Roman Empire. The prevailing Roman view of wealth said that each person had a right to do with his wealth whatever he chose. Apparently, few Christians in Corinth (the wealthy anyway) felt any obligation to care for other members of the church.

But the Roman way was not the Jesus way—something the Corinthians needed to learn. Badly!

You can see the implication of this dreadful Corinthian ignorance when the people gathered for a regular event meant to rehearse the core themes of the Christian gospel: Jesus's death and resurrection.

The Lord's Supper was supposed to be a fellowship meal marked with brotherly love, unity, reverence, and joy. But it didn't work that way in Corinth. There, at the table of the Lord, affluent people apparently gorged themselves with food and drink befitting a five-star restaurant, while the poor ate little or nothing.

The situation bothered Paul enough that he dedicated a significant part of his letter to this group's selfishness when he wrote to the congregation. He was outraged at such absurd, un-Christlike behavior. No full-life generosity here!

Paul was quite aware of what the lack of a generous spirit was doing to this potentially powerful church. It was splitting the congregation, and it was shriveling the souls of so-called Christians who had the ability to make life better for others but chose to do nothing. Paul must have felt deeply defensive of those who were ignored and so completely humiliated.

Call this a massive breakdown in full-life generosity. The evidence was right there at the table, where people were supposed to be reflecting upon the sacrificial love of Jesus at the cross.

Perhaps we cannot fully grasp this spectacle of insensitivity from a distance of so many centuries. You may ask: *how could people be so insensitive, so careless, so lacking in love for one another?*

But could it be that the same attitude of selfishness lurks at the door of our own lives or in some of our contemporary congregations? Is it possible that we are just a bit more subtle in how we go about dividing the rich and the poor? Does the Corinthian spirit still show itself today?

What would Scrooge say if he were invited to speak to this gathering of Corinthian people? Would there have been tears in his eyes? Fire in his soul? Busy hands as he emptied his pockets to match the needs of those he saw so completely ignored?

Ebenezer asks: Would you care to be a member of this church? And if you were, what would you say to its people?

Reflection: How easy is it for any of us to look past the needy people right in front of us? In our churches? In our neighborhoods?

BeScrooged Activity: The Bible says that God's people are to be mindful of those who are "weak." Who might that be in your world? Try to make a list of five to seven groups of people who live within a reasonable distance of your home or church who, in your opinion, fit this category. What sort of needs may they have?

DAY 6:
IT'S ALL ABOUT THE HEART

READ LUKE 18:18-30

"You still lack one thing. Sell everything you have and give to the poor, and you will have treasure in heaven. Then come, follow me." (Luke 18:22)

"He fashions a god and worships it; he makes an idol and bows down to it…
He prays to it and says, 'Save me; you are my god.'…He feeds on ashes,
a deluded heart misleads him; he cannot save himself, or say, 'Is not this thing in
my right hand a lie?'" (Excerpts from Isaiah 44:15-20).

WE'RE NOT TOLD HIS NAME, BUT WE DO KNOW THAT HE WAS WELL-CONNECTED, influential, and financially advantaged. He was also smart, clever, and curious.

As he approached Jesus, he said he had a question for him. That question—*What must I do to inherit eternal life?*—does not seem contrived. The man was clearly measuring Jesus, considering whether or not he should ask to join his band of followers.

Jesus's first answer: *You know the commandments; keep them!*

You can imagine the disciples hanging on every word of this conversation. Common sense suggests that they would want this "celebrity" on their disciple-team. His presence, they might reason, would doubtless influence others to join Jesus's new movement. Just having him around would upgrade the respectability of Jesus's mission.

You can picture the disciples already salivating over how this man's influence and economic resources might support their long-range plans. So it's probable that the disciples listened intently, hoping Jesus would say the right things and convince this young man to sign up.

"I've kept all the commandments…since my youth," the man said when Jesus spoke of keeping the commandments.

Mark, one of the three gospel writers who recounts this story, says, "Jesus looked at him and loved him." What in the world does that mean? Probably that he was not a bad man. He had good intentions. His seeking an association with Jesus was sincere.

We can imagine that Jesus would have dearly loved to include this bright young man among his disciples. But there was one thing on which he would not compromise: this man's attitude toward his wealth and material assets. That's significant!

"There's one thing you have left to do," the Lord interjected.

Perhaps the disciples drew in closer so they would miss nothing. Jesus's next words would likely determine how this deal would go down.

"Go sell everything you have…give it to the poor…then come and follow."

Were the Lord's disciples incredulous when they heard these words? Had Jesus actually told his man to divest his holdings and then give the money away, not keep even a smidgen for the little community of disciples to use? Was this the best answer the Lord could devise?

Soon after Jesus's comment, the young man walked away…sad. You may wonder what he was thinking. Did he say to himself, "It was all going in the right direction until he raised the matter of possessions and money?" Both he and the Lord's disciples must have thought, "Why did Jesus have to ask the young man to sacrifice so much?"

Answer: Because part of following Jesus—and it's not a small part—requires a new strategy, a strategy that begins to reshape and transform our hearts and allows us to live out a generous gospel in exciting and sacrificial ways.

The faith of a growing disciple cannot be influenced by a care for money, possessions, other earthly idols, or anything that distracts us and takes the "place" of God in our lives. Jesus did not surround himself with the rich *because* they were rich. He welcomed those to his side who were prepared to accept him as Lord and master and who were not controlled by their material holdings or destructive idols. Unfortunately, the young man in this story could not let go.

Ebenezer asks: Do you know people like the young man, who struggle with the idol of money and material things? Is this a struggle for you?

Reflection: In I Samuel 6:17, it says: "The Lord does not look at the things people look at. People look at the outward appearance, but the Lord looks at the heart." How do this Bible passage and the story of the young man speak to you and the condition of your own heart?

BeScrooged Activity: Idols can be "religious objects" made of stone, wood, or metal. But idols can also take on other forms. What "idols" might interfere with your ability to follow

Christ at a greater level of obedience? Here are some examples that we might struggle with and might take the place of God. How do your spouse and friends respond to this list as well? What are their idols?

Examples:
- I tend to enjoy gaining control, power, or influence over others in my world.
- I seek things that bring me pleasure and "comfort" as much as possible in my life.
- I am preoccupied with the pursuit of security for myself, my spouse, or my children.
- I am driven or distracted by issues of lust in my life.
- I make every effort to please people so they will like me.
- I am very conscious of my physical appearance before others.
- I am addicted to…
- I am preoccupied with accumulating things that that increase my status in life.
- I will do anything to enhance my career.
- I want people to be impressed with my intelligence.
- I never feel as if I have enough money.

Take a moment and list your top one to three "idols" in their order of importance to you. You might want to have a dialogue with a friend or your spouse about each other's lists. How does each one threaten to come between you and God's call to be a fully generous person?

DAY 7:
OPPORTUNITIES AT THE DOORSTEP

READ LUKE 16:19-31

"He looked up and saw Abraham far away, with Lazarus by his side. So he called to him, 'Father Abraham, have pity on me and send Lazarus to dip the tip of his finger in the water and cool my tongue, because I am in agony in this fire.'" (Luke 16:23)

JESUS TOLD A STORY ABOUT TWO MEN (ONE VERY WEALTHY, the other very poor) who lived out their lives just feet away from each other. Just a few feet!

The first man, the one who lived large, was a fastidious dresser and ate very, very well. We're also told that he was insensitive to human need, even when it was evident just outside his front door.

The second man, Lazarus, could not have been more destitute. Sick, hungry, abandoned at the gate of the other man's mansion, he was left to hope each day that someone would take pity on him and do something to relieve his suffering. It appears as if the dogs in the neighborhood were more attentive to him than were the human beings.

So far, this is not a happy story.

In painting a word picture of these two men, Jesus was at his storytelling best. In just a few sentences, he captured the attention of his listeners as he described the contrasts in how the two men lived. Who wouldn't feel contempt for the first man and compassion for the second?

Jesus's story then moves on to a time when their lives were judged. The Lord seems to ask, "Do you ever wonder what happens when men like these two have to face God and account for their choices in life?"

When Lazarus died, Jesus said, he was *lifted to heaven* (lifted!) by angels and assigned a place next to Israel's most honored patriarch, Abraham. By placing Lazarus next to Abraham, Jesus was making an important point. He wanted everyone to visualize Lazarus the beggar in a position of high honor.

Then, speaking of the death of the rich man, Jesus said little more than that he was buried. Buried! There is no question as to where Jesus's sympathies lay.

The rest of the Lord's story is startling. It takes place in hell.

The rich man, now dead, found himself in a place of chronic suffering, a place so horrific that the once best-dressed connoisseur was reduced to begging (note the reversal in roles) for just a drop of water—and that, if possible, from the tip of Lazarus's finger.

The conclusion of what Jesus had to say was grim. In effect, the rich man was told that it was too late for him to hope for anything. Having shown no generosity in life, he would receive no generosity in the next.

You can be sure everyone listened to this story with great thoughtfulness.

When it comes to greed, to stinginess, to selfishness, a story is never over until we see it in its final, eternal perspective. Jesus's lesson is that faith can be demonstrated in economic terms. That he who is on the bottom here on earth may be placed on the top in heaven. Oh...and that he who *thought* he was first in this life may be last somewhere else.

Ebenezer asks: How does Jesus build up the contrasts between these two men? What point he is trying to make? Do we overlook, ignore, or neglect certain kinds of people in our world? If so, who might they be?

Reflection: If you were to draw a three-mile circle around your house or the church where you worship, who could you compare to the man in the dirt just outside the rich man's home? What do you perceive to be their greatest needs?

BeScrooged Activity: Identify the most provocative themes that have emerged in your readings and reflections this week. Ask God to open your eyes to some brand-new opportunities to act generously in the next few days.

You can get an early start on next week's activities if you take a look at Ebenezer's Generosity Ladder on the next page. Discover where you are on the ladder and begin deepening your full-life generosity story.

EBENEZER'S LADDER

THIS WEEK OF READINGS HIGHLIGHTED SEVEN SCROOGE-LIKE PEOPLE in the Bible who, in various ways, made the acquisition of power, wealth, and leisure into a form of idol worship. The idea of full-life generosity–that the totality of one's life and possessions belong to God and are meant to serve his purposes—never occurred to them.

St. Paul, concerned about such human propensities, wrote, "Command those who are rich in this present world not to be arrogant nor *to put their hope in wealth*, which is so uncertain, but to put their hope in God, who richly provides us with everything for our enjoyment. *Command them to do good, to be rich in good deeds, and to be generous and willing to share. In this way they will lay up treasure for themselves as a firm foundation for the coming age, so that they may take hold of the life that is truly life.*" (I Timothy 6:17-19, emphasis ours)

Clearly, Paul was passionate that Christ-followers might come to an understanding of what we are calling full-life generosity. If you examine his remarks, you'll find that he was interested in much more than money. Being "rich in good deeds" suggests that generosity involves one's character, skills, compassion, and possessions. Becoming a person who embodies those things is no simple task.

In our attempt to study this "transformational generosity," we wanted to provide a way to evaluate our own individual journeys. Through years of work in the Christian generosity sector, an illustration began to take shape that is now known as Ebenezer's Ladder. We've used this spiritual formation tool for a few years now to benchmark where we as Christians may be in our mindsets and attitudes toward generosity.

At its core, Ebenezer's Ladder helps us see how we make generous or ungenerous decisions. Are our decisions focused on the kingdom of God? Are they selfless or selfish? What are the key biblical values that drive us as generous people? What is our view of God? Is he Lord of all we have and all we are?

The structure is fairly straightforward. Not surprisingly, the bottom rung of Ebenezer's Ladder represents a perspective that is resistant to generosity. As the ladder progresses, things begin to change. Each rung identifies our various motivations and approaches, which lead us to make common everyday decisions that reflect the depth of our generosity. As we climb up or down a ladder, so we Christians can ascend or descend in our passion for a fully generous life that drives us closer or further from Jesus as the center point of our choices and lives.

We'll look more in depth at each rung on the ladder in the following pages and in the pages following Week 2's devotionals. Our initial exploration will include the bottom four rungs, whose attitudes are tough and oftentimes uncomfortable to contemplate. The important thing to remember is that full-life generosity has its ups and downs—and it is not unusual for each of us to climb a rung or two during some seasons of our spiritual journey and then, inadvertently, to descend a bit.

The Seven Rungs of Ebenezer's Ladder

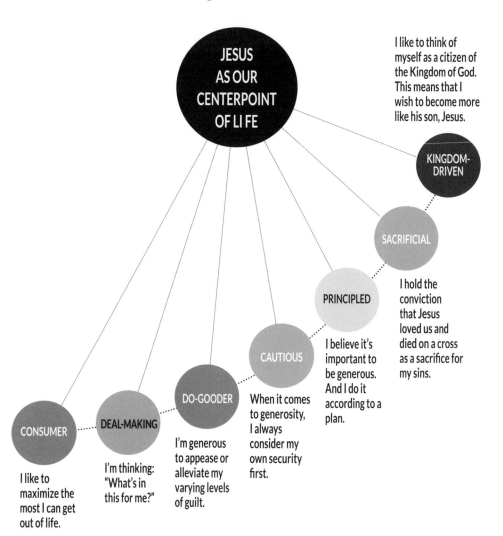

JESUS AS OUR CENTERPOINT OF LIFE

I like to think of myself as a citizen of the Kingdom of God. This means that I wish to become more like his son, Jesus.

KINGDOM-DRIVEN

SACRIFICIAL

I hold the conviction that Jesus loved us and died on a cross as a sacrifice for my sins.

PRINCIPLED

I believe it's important to be generous. And I do it according to a plan.

CAUTIOUS

When it comes to generosity, I always consider my own security first.

DO-GOODER

I'm generous to appease or alleviate my varying levels of guilt.

DEAL-MAKING

I'm thinking: "What's in this for me?"

CONSUMER

I like to maximize the most I can get out of life.

1. CONSUMER

I understand that people think my approach to life is somewhat selfish, but I have to look after myself. I want to maximize all that life can offer—without all the hindrances people or religion might put on me. I've got a strong case of fear of missing out (FOMA). I like the finer things in life if I can afford them and work hard on shaping my status in my community or at work. I strive to build upon my own personal and/or family brand.

My home, my cars, my family's status, my business position, and my plan to rise to the top: they're meant to make a statement about how successful I am and how comfortable I want to be. I see all those things as a way to make me happier.

I'm usually a private person. I do not invite many people in. I struggle valuing relationships in my life and tend to be more transactional with them. awkward

I think loving people and serving people is a nice thing to do, but it is not one of my priorities. I only offer myself or my resources in a generous way if it won't take up too much of my time, or if it will improve my personal brand or how people see me. I've worked hard and give myself the credit for my success.

I don't tend to make God a priority in my life, and when I do I perceive him to be more as Santa Claus God (gift giver).

2. DEAL-MAKING

I've always been a little cynical about giving my money and things to others. It sounds good in theory, but I tend to only be generous when I feel social pressure around me. (I see giving as an obligation.) It's really not something that is a priority in my life.

The challenge is that I feel like I'm constantly being nagged. (Sometimes I feel like people *demand* that I give my time and money—and once I'm asked too many times, I lose interest in giving at all.) At the same time, when I do get involved in certain efforts and giving campaigns, I believe those efforts can help me with my social status in certain contexts.

Overall, I am kind and sympathetic toward the unfortunate around me. I have strong values, but they don't usually inspire me to do more than give here and there. I love the public praise I get in the community or in church for the things I do and give, but I don't have much passion for more than that.

I know my attitude might bother people, because I may come across as wondering "What's in it for me?" when I'm asked to be generous. If you want me to give my time, my experience, and my money, what will I get in return? My name on a building or a clean water well in Africa? I've worked hard and earned all I have. I need to protect it and keep on investing it. I guess that may be the way I approach God as well. I would much rather see him as my "rabbit's foot" in life.

3. DO-GOODER

I enjoy doing things for people and chipping in when I can. I like the way I feel when I'm helping people and can see the joy on their faces, but my level of personal or financial commitment could be perceived as minimal. My idea of generosity is mainly about "doing" good things and less about giving financially. Most of what I give is spontaneous or based on a spiked emotion, but is often not carefully considered. You could call my generosity somewhat *whimsical* and certainly not strategic.

Quite frankly, I get involved in activities that are offered because I feel guilty when I don't participate or contribute. I tend to have a pretty strong social conscience and a heart for certain things in my community, my church, or the world. I measure my generosity by how much "good" I think I'm doing (enough). At times I compare my generosity to that of my friends, other families, and colleagues.

I believe God is pleased with my willingness to do "good things." (I struggle with the concept of how my "works" and generosity will get me better status in heaven.)

4. CAUTIOUS

I enjoy being generous in many ways and feel great when I'm thinking of others before myself. However, I struggle with feeling that I need to be careful with how generous I am. I have my limits and am cautious with what I have. I'm never sure I have enough, and I don't want to lose my security in life right now.

I don't mind writing a check now and then. When I give, I get a rush of excitement. I like to pay for meals when I'm with family and friends, but I do have a habit of keeping score. I expect people to reciprocate. The structured side of me really doesn't want to get involved with people and situations beyond my comfort zone. I help my friends on certain projects, fundraising efforts, and campaigns, but I can't do too much.

Most folks perceive me as a private person since I'm reluctant to open up my life. My spouse would like to host more group dinners or invite new people who need encouragement to our house. But I prefer to keep my guard up because I don't feel like I have much to give to others, nor the time to offer anyone beyond my family and closest friends.

I know God will provide for all my needs, but I still get fearful about decision making. Sometimes my financial struggles drive my inability to be generous. It hurts me at times that I don't have the resources or time to help. I know I ought to be generous, but I have a tough time seeing past my limitations and fear of giving too much and losing my security down the road. I don't want to depend on others and be a burden. Therefore, I'm pretty calculating in my giving.

Where You Land on the Ladder

For a moment, visualize yourself—even though you may be repelled—at the first rung—the *Taker* rung—of Ebenezer's Ladder. Note the comments that characterize people who are associated with this lowest of the categories. Admittedly, there is nothing attractive about this rung.

Then go to the second rung, then the third and the rest. Somewhere there will be a rung that you feel describes most accurately the kind of generosity or non-generosity that marks you at this moment in life.

When you have settled on the rung that best describes you, ask what it would take for you to climb one rung higher.

WEEK TWO

WE'VE TAKEN A LOOK AT SEVEN "SCROOGE-TYPES." Each of them seems to have had a particular blind spot regarding a form of selfishness that was never overcome. Each desperately needed BeScroogement, an awakening to full-life generosity.

Now that we've examined their lives, what about a look in the opposite direction? Jesus was the personification of full-life generosity. How did the Lord do it? He focused on generous people. He told stories about generosity. He taught the principles of generosity. And when he was through, more than a few people had their eyes opened to a whole new way of life.

But first, we will return to the story of Ebenezer Scrooge and his journey toward BeScroogement.

In this second section of Ebenezer's journey, the issue is intervention. What Scrooge needed more than anything was someone who was prepared to look him square in the eye and force him to face the reality of what he'd become. He also needed someone who could convince him to see the direction in which his life was headed.

Who better to take on this task than his former, long-dead business partner, Jacob Marley? Quite possibly Marley is the only person to whom Scrooge might listen. For one thing, they shared a similar history of business activity and obsession with the accumulation of money. Scrooge would quickly recognize that Marley's destiny was soon to be his own if something didn't change. Cratchit, Scrooge's nephew Fred, and various well-meaning people in the neighborhood might try to reason with Scrooge. But they were likely to get nowhere with him. Jacob Marley? He's got influence with Scrooge. Watch how that influence slowly works its way into Scrooge's heart.

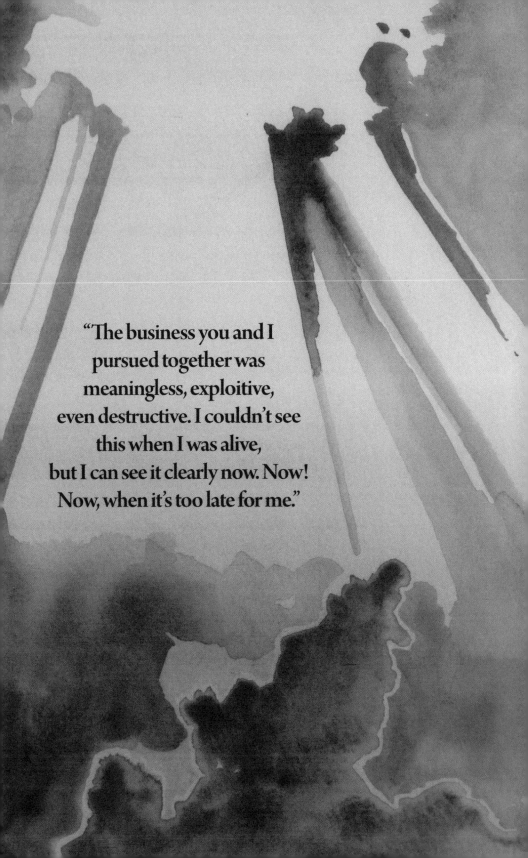

"The business you and I
pursued together was
meaningless, exploitive,
even destructive. I couldn't see
this when I was alive,
but I can see it clearly now. Now!
Now, when it's too late for me."

Intervention: Climbing Ebenezer's Ladder

At 7:00 p.m. on that memorable Christmas Eve (not a minute earlier), Bob Cratchit and I put away our work and headed for the front door of the offices of Scrooge and Marley. Because of the nastiness of our earlier conversation about Christmas Day, we were not on speaking terms as we stepped outside. You might have expected that Cratchit would say, "Boss, I hope you have a good day tomorrow." And you might have anticipated that I would say, "Bob, here's a little Christmas bonus to put under your tree."

But that didn't happen.

Cratchit quickly wrapped a small blanket around his shoulders and started down the street toward his home and family. The further he went, the faster he walked until he broke into a run as if he couldn't wait to get home. Soon, he was out of sight.

Recalling that moment these many years later, I'm struck with the fact that it never occurred to me to question why this man, with whom I'd worked every day for years, had no coat to protect himself from the miserably cold and damp weather. That insensitivity is just one example of the kind of man I was. Think of it: I, Ebenezer Scrooge, the wealthiest man on the block, could read the balance sheet of any company and gain an idea of its worth in a matter of minutes. Yet I was completely oblivious to the physical needs of my one employee.

When Cratchit had disappeared, I turned in the opposite direction and headed for a dreary pub, where I ate a tasteless meal and reviewed the day's receivables. You may wonder why I chose a pub for dinner on Christmas Eve night. The answer is simple: there was no one for me to go home to. No one who'd prepared a home-cooked dinner. No one who would want to hear about my day. Obviously, the Cratchit home and the Scrooge "home" were totally different places.

Later, when I reached the front door of the building where I lived (or slept, anyway), I experienced the first of a string of unnerving surprises that would occur that evening. While putting my key in the lock, I thought I saw the ashen, expressionless face of Jacob Marley, my one-time business partner, reflected on the door knocker. Mind you, by this time the man had been dead for seven years, but there he was, his eyes staring, looking straight through me.

When I saw Marley's face, I trembled. My heart began beating furiously. The face remained in place on the knocker for just a few seconds, long enough to get my full attention, and then it faded away. It was all I could do to open the door and secure the several locks from the inside. Lighting a candle, I felt compelled to begin a frantic search to ensure no one besides me was there. After checking every room and closet on the main floor, I climbed the stairs to the second floor.

There, I started searching all over again. For who, for what? I have no idea. I just rushed from room to room, looking for anything suspicious. But nothing seemed out of place. I found no one in the closets, no one behind the doors, no one under the furniture. So, after checking everything, I went to my bedroom, double-bolted the door, and prepared for bed.

I tried hard to forget what I had seen at the front door. Maybe I was just getting old, I told myself. Sure, that was it. I was just getting old, and old people have fantasies like that. With such thoughts I calmed myself, and my heart began to beat normally again.

Then came a second surprise. While I was changing into my nightclothes, Marley's face appeared again, this time on the wall above the fireplace. At the same time a bell began to ring, then another, and another. Soon it seemed as if dozens of bells were clanging, clanging, clanging. And then I began to hear a hideous noise from somewhere downstairs, as if heavy chains were being dragged across a floor.

The face on the wall, the bells, the chains. How can I describe the terror that began to surge within me? I was frantic, frozen with fear. Normally, I was the man who controlled everything around him. But in this moment I controlled nothing. I was the controlled.

Then, just when it seemed that things couldn't get worse, Jacob Marley crashed through the bedroom door. This time it was not a face on a door knocker or a fireplace wall that haunted me, but a life-sized Marley. Oh, he was a revolting sight! The first thing about him that caught my eye was the chain wrapped around and around his body, one end of it dragging behind him like a tail.

"Why are you here?" was the only thing I could think to say when I was able to speak.

Marley responded, " It is necessary that the spirit of every man travel the world and see those things he may never have wished to see. If he refuses to do this during his lifetime (as you and I refused, Ebenezer), he is compelled to do it later, when his life has ended. I am on that journey now."

At the time I didn't appreciate the significance of Marley's words, but I do today. Marley was right: we had never traveled the world. In fact, we knew very little about our own hometown. If we went out, it was only in the pursuit of business. A sense of concern or interest in the larger world or its people (unless they were customers) had never been a priority.

Now Marley was saying that we could not have been more wrong. We should have been more aware of the people around us. Maybe we should have reached out to all kinds of people, to educate ourselves in the depth and breadth of human need.

When I asked Marley to explain the chain he was dragging, he said, "This chain took a lifetime to forge. Every link represents the selfish choices I made in life. And *you*, Ebenezer, will someday drag a chain much longer and heavier than this one. Already you have lived seven more years than I did, and what have you done with these years? You've thought only about yourself."

"Jacob, you're frightening me!" I cried out. "Is this the only thing you can say to me?"

I was hoping that Marley might begin to reminisce about our partnership, the money we'd made, the real estate holdings we'd owned. Had he completely forgotten about all of this? Was our success no longer important to him?

But Marley wasn't about to change his tune.

"I have no hope for you, Ebenezer Scrooge," he said. "If there is anything redemptive in your future, it will have to come from others. But you can be sure that it won't come from me."

I tried flattering him.

"Jacob," I said, "you were once the best in the business." But my words seemed only to send him into a greater rage.

"Business?" he shouted. "You want to talk about being the best in business? Listen to me, Ebenezer Scrooge. The suffering of mankind should have been my business. Giving away assets, not hoarding them, should have been my business. Opening my home to others should have been my business. Coming alongside people who were hungry and sick, engaging those whose lives were broken, advocating for people who were victims of injustice. All of these acts would have been a noble business."

Unfortunately for me, Marley wasn't through.

"The business you and I pursued together was meaningless, exploitive, even destructive. I couldn't see this when I was alive, but I can see it clearly now. Now! Now, when it's too late for me."

Marley's words exploded like a bomb in my heart. What could I say? The man had just condemned everything I'd ever lived for. No one had ever spoken to me like this before.

Finally, Marley quieted down. He indicated that it was time for him to go. As he began to disappear, he said I had but one chance to turn my life around and escape a fate similar to his.

"Tonight, you will be visited by three spirits."

"Three spirits," he repeated. Each, he explained, would force me to take a hard look at certain seasons of my life. They would point out my selfishness, my lack of compassion, my failure to be generous. If I listened to them, he said, I just might learn some things that would change me forever.

Looking back, I now understand that Marley was introducing me to the process of BeScrooge-ment.

Today, I remember that conversation and give thanks that Marley was so honest with me. I have come to believe that some, if not all of us, need the kind of confrontation I had that night with my old partner, Jacob Marley—a moment when we are forced to face truths about ourselves that we've long avoided.

> **Ebenezer asks:**
> Scrooge says, "All of us need the kind of confrontation I had that night with my old partner, Jacob Marley." Has there ever been a moment in your spiritual journey when you found it necessary to evaluate your patterns of generosity? What did you learn about yourself? Have you remained faithful to the message that came to you in that moment?

I like to call such a visitation a *Marley moment,* or a *breaking* experience. Alcoholics I have known speak of it as "hitting the bottom." Call it what you will, all of us need to examine ourselves and ask if we need to be freed from the stubbornness, arrogance, defensiveness, or rage that prohibits us from yielding to the truth of who we are and what God wants to make us into—people transformed, converted from selfishness to a generous kind of living.

DAY 8:
IT'S ALL GOD'S, NOT MINE

READ LUKE 21:1-4

"As Jesus looked up, he saw the rich putting their gifts into the temple treasury. He also saw a poor widow put in two very small copper coins. "Truly I tell you," he said, "this poor widow has put in more than all the others. All these people gave their gifts out of their wealth; but she out of her poverty put in all she had to live on."

IT HAPPENED SO QUICKLY AND QUIETLY THAT NO ONE PAID A BIT OF ATTENTION. No one, that is, except Jesus. And what he saw turned into a memorable teaching experience for his disciples. Many generations later, we are still profiting from what happened in that moment.

The time: a few days before the Lord would be arrested and crucified. The location: that place in the Jerusalem temple where people dropped their tithes and offerings into huge trumpet-shaped receptacles. The scene: a crowd of people pushing and shoving one another as each person attempted to convey that his offering was the largest.

To these self-promoting religious celebrities, Jesus paid scant attention. His eyes were fixed on an impoverished widow who was quietly waiting for her turn to place her offering in the treasury.

It's possible that Jesus had been expecting her, for he immediately pointed her out to his disciples. One can almost hear him saying, "Gentlemen, watch this woman carefully. You're about to learn something that means nothing to the crowd but everything to my Father in heaven. What others might ignore, he will always remember."

The men watched as the widow stealthily dropped two of the smallest coins in the receptacle and disappeared. Think about it! That "micro-gift" and her humble way of giving it gained the attention of the Son of God.

"This woman," the Lord said, "has given more than anyone else."

What could that mean? More than anyone else? Can you imagine the consternation those words must have caused the disciples?

The widow and her gift represent a new way of measuring generosity. Her giving was powerful because her heart was pure. The gifts of the rich were loud and flashy, but hardly selfless or sacrificial. The gift of the widow, though small in amount, was enormous in another dimension. As Jesus said, "[S]he gave all she had."

Let's review. Most people in the temple that morning gave because giving was required and because it provided an opportunity for "self-promotion." Their giving, they thought, was a way to bring attention to themselves and how righteous they were.

The widow, on the other hand, paid little attention to what other people thought. She gave out of her sincere desire to worship the God of Israel. She believed God had been generous to her, so she would be generous to him. And, of course, she intended that her gift would ultimately benefit others.

This incident had to be one of the disciples' most important learning experiences in their years with the Master. It must have provoked a lot of conversation about the meaning of giving and its centrality in a life of faith.

The widow's generosity mirrors the pattern of God's generosity. He revealed his generous nature when he gave his son Jesus to the world. God's generosity awakens the heart with the question, "If my Father in heaven has given his best for me, what should I be giving back to him?"

The economics of heaven stand in great contrast to those of mankind. Left to our own devices, we usually begin with the question, "What's the least I can get away with?" Heaven suggests an alternative question: *What is the most I can do?*

The widow gave the most she could. No one saw this more clearly than Jesus. When others opted for public adulation and a religious reputation, he looked away. When she gave, he noticed and offered heavenly approval. That woman will surely occupy a place of honor in heaven.

Ebenezer Asks: Most gifts are appraised in terms of numerical value, but how did Jesus measure the gift of the unnamed woman? What did Jesus want his disciples to learn? In what way is this story an indictment on institutional religion?

Reflection: Return to Ebenezer's Ladder and find the rung that you think corresponds to the widow in this story.

BeScrooged Activity: Check your motivations. Be open to giving generously today without being noticed (behind the scenes) and test yourself and challenge your motives. Does it mean more when you give anonymously and it's between you and God and no one else knows?

DAY 9:
JESUS AND THE SIMPLE GOSPEL

READ MATTHEW 19:13-15

"Then people brought little children to Jesus for him to place his hands on them and pray for them. But the disciples rebuked them. Jesus said, 'Let the little children come to me, and do not hinder them, for the kingdom of heaven belongs to such as these.'"
(Matthew 19:13-14)

THE SCRIPTURES GIVE US A WONDERFUL PICTURE OF JESUS'S LOVE for children and what they meant to him. So what does it say about the disciples of our Lord when they turned away mothers and infants who sought the blessing, the generosity, of the Son of God? Perhaps this is one of those moments when the twelve companions of the Lord had something important to learn about the full-life generous spirit.

It appears as if the disciples assumed Jesus would prefer to engage with *important people* who approached him on religious business. It was perfectly logical, then, for them to block the way of children.

That was a big mistake. What these men had yet to learn was the uniqueness in the way Jesus saw human beings—through the eyes of full-life generosity.

From Jesus's perspective, children were more likely to appreciate the simplicity and purity of his gospel than many adults. Jesus welcomed children to his side because he knew they would open themselves to the truth of the things he taught.

Thus, Jesus rebuked his disciples when he saw what they were doing. "Let the little children come to me," he insisted.

Full-life generosity emanates from a heart that sees and celebrates the value of every human being. It means having eyes that seek out the weaker and more vulnerable among us.

Jesus was rarely drawn to the busy or powerful people in his world. Perhaps he did not wish to expend energy on those who thought they already had all the answers. Why should he spend time with people who resisted the notion that their lives were broken? Children, on the other hand, were teachable, and they discerned the freedom and the joy that could come from living a kingdom-style life. Simplicity and humility always trump pride and the promotion of ego in the eyes of Jesus.

The disciples had yet to learn this new way of engaging with people. Until the twelve understood Jesus's full-life generous spirit, their attention would always be drawn to the powerful and the privileged. Perhaps, many years later, some of them looked back on this moment and thought, "So that's what he was trying to say: serve the children and the childlike first."

Ebenezer Asks: What is it about children that attracted Jesus's attention? What might have caused the disciples to think children were insignificant?

Reflection: How can we develop a better lens so we see the childlike, vulnerable, or hurting lives around us?

BeScrooged Activity: We all need to practice the simple, childlike generosity that this story illustrates. How can we be free, consistent, and unbounded by the opportunities to be generous that come into our daily lives? Find two to three ways today to respond with a childlike freedom to the opportunities you encounter.

DAY 10:
WHAT DOES A CHANGED PERSON LOOK LIKE?

READ MARK 5:1-20

"When they came to Jesus, they saw the man who had been possessed by the legion of demons, sitting there, dressed and in his right mind." (Mark 5:15)

THE ONLY NAME WE HAVE FOR HIM IS LEGION, a name he either took for himself or was given after he went, well, crazy. His family name and the details of his earlier life are unknown to us. We are left to wonder if he'd been married. Was he a father? Had he ever held any kind of job? Could he have been at one time a respected member of the community? For these questions, we have no answers.

What we do know is that somewhere along the way he lost any semblance of self-control and became destructive. You may wonder what people thought as they tried to keep their distance from him. Did they have memories of good times with him in the past? Did they hope, one day, he might come to his senses and rejoin the community? Or had they given up hope?

Things apparently got worse as time passed. Finally, some in the community tried to physically restrain him, but nothing worked for long. Sooner or later, he always managed to break loose.

The gospel writers describe this man's behavior as suggestive of the presence of evil demons in his life.

Then one day Jesus visited the region, and the first person he ran into was this mad man. While most of us would have backed away, Jesus engaged him. This is redemptive generosity in action.

The subject of their conversation concerned the evil powers within the man that had stripped away his humanity. Perhaps he and the Lord also spoke of the others who were affected by this tragedy—his family, neighbors, and those with whom he once worked.

If there was more to their conversation, we don't know about it, but we do read that there came a moment when Jesus accomplished what no one else had been able to do. He poured the power of heaven into this man. Instantly, he had new life.

And the demons? When Jesus forced them out of the man, they entered a herd of swine (two thousand pigs), which stampeded down a hill and drowned in the lake of Galilee. Admittedly, it's a strange story. But that's the way Mark, the author, and others saw it.

The fact that a man's life had been reclaimed seems not to have impressed the owners of the doomed livestock, because when they arrived, they demanded that the Lord leave. The word *generous* would hardly apply to their attitude or regard for their personal interests.

In the end, the community cared more for its loss of pigs than the salvation and healing of this man. These people epitomize the ugliness of greed.

See this newly transformed man in your imagination. He sits quietly (now at peace), clothed (now possessing dignity), and in his right mind (now able to think and feel). This is a beautiful picture of what the generous, redemptive power of Jesus Christ can accomplish. Soon this man will return to his family and friends. He will travel the region telling the story of how Jesus gave him back his life. He epitomizes the power of a generosity that is expressed by giving mercy, rescuing the desperate, and redeeming the lost.

Ebenezer Asks: Why are the local residents so disturbed over what Jesus has done for this man? What does that indicate about their attitude toward full-life generosity? What are the results of Jesus's redemptive effort on behalf of this man?

Reflection: Consider making a list of up to five people whose lives seem to be damaged beyond repair. Commit to praying for these people on a daily basis, that the generous love of Christ might cause a seemingly impossible transformation.

BeScrooged Activity: Identify one or two ways you can encourage or help someone who is in a desperate position and needs you to act redemptively on their behalf. The key is to look and listen for opportunities. Don't hesitate to jump out of your comfort zone.

DAY 11:
LOOKING AT A BROKEN WORLD WITH NEW EYES

READ LUKE 10:25-37

"A man was going down from Jerusalem to Jericho, when he was attacked by robbers. They stripped him of his clothes, beat him, and went away, leaving him half dead." (Luke 10:30)

A TRAVELER ON THE ROAD BETWEEN JERUSALEM AND JERICHO was mugged by thieves. Brutally mugged and left for dead. Another traveler, the Samaritan, came to his aid and saved his life.

The story actually begins with two leaders from the world of organized religion who, one after the other, spotted the victim but pretended he didn't exist. Moving to the other side of the road, each reasoned, "If I don't *get close to him*, he is not my responsibility."

Did these two men think themselves too busy? Were they reluctant to soil their clothes? Did they fear the thieves were still nearby, and they could also be mugged if they lingered? Or is it possible that they concluded the victim wasn't deserving of their attention, that they were not expected to help someone beneath their social class?

After them comes the Samaritan. Most of the people listening to Jesus that day despised Samaritans, and we can almost feel them stiffen when they realize where this story is going. "Anyone but a Samaritan," someone might have complained.

Yes, it was a Samaritan, Jesus said, who in the spirit of full-life generosity went to the dying man. He saw him, took pity on him, and bandaged his wounds. He poured oil and wine on the wounds to prevent infection. He lifted the man onto his donkey, cared for him at an inn, and left money with the innkeeper to provide further care. Finally, he promised to return to see if anything more needed to be done. He overlooked nothing in caring for this stranger.

This story of the Samaritan's sacrificial actions highlights the place of compassion in full-life generosity. A man from a hated culture sees a broken human in the ditch and knows what he must do. And Jesus affirms it all.

The other two men who'd gotten there first may have been religious champions in Jerusalem's temple life. But out on the road, when faced with danger, inconvenience, and a certain messiness, they were useless.

Upon which of these travelers does God smile? That was Jesus's point.

Ebenezer Asks: What are some of the extremes to which Jesus goes in telling this story? Do you think Jesus is being excessive when he paints the religious figures as callous and uninvolved? What does the Samaritan have to teach us as we watch him turn his attention to the man in the ditch?

Reflection: Where would you place the Good Samaritan on Ebenezer's Ladder? Where would you put the two temple personalities? What social mores or physical barriers in your world may prevent you from reaching out to those in need?

BeScrooged Activity: Reflect: Last week we introduced you to Ebenezer's Ladder. Begin extending your current generosity story by finding ways to encourage yourself up the ladder. Record the ways you have exhibited generosity today. Does generosity come naturally to you? Why or why not? Are you moving up the ladder?

DAY 12:
WHO TOUCHED ME?

READ MARK 5:21-43

"A large crowd followed and pressed around him. And a woman was there who had been subject to bleeding for twelve years. She had suffered a great deal under the care of many doctors and had spent all she had, yet instead of getting better she grew worse. When she heard about Jesus, she came up behind him in the crowd and touched his cloak... Immediately her bleeding stopped....At once Jesus realized that power had gone out from him. He turned around in the crowd and asked, "Who touched my clothes?" (Mark 5:24-30)

PICTURE A WILD CROWD. AT ITS CENTER: JESUS AND HIS DISCIPLES. In the middle of this rush-hour mess, there is a desperate woman on a personal mission. She seeks healing.

We do not know this woman's name, but the gospel writers tell us that she had been afflicted with a debilitating blood disease for twelve years.

Because of her illness, she could not be touched by others, could not enter a house of worship, and could not participate in the common life of the community. The oft-used religious word that indicated her condition was *unclean*.

Always in search of a cure, this woman had spent herself into bankruptcy with no positive results. As time went on she grew more and more hopeless.

Now she has learned Jesus is in the area. She must have been aware of his reputation as a healer because she said to herself, "If I just touch his clothes, I will be healed." There's an interesting confidence in these words.

Touch his clothes. That was her only hope, for no woman in her culture was permitted to physically touch any man except her own husband or her male children. So this touch had to be limited to his clothes. To the edge of his clothes, the fringe. Nothing else. Also, no one must notice that the touch has occurred. Quite a risky venture, some might say.

But her scheme was successful. When she reached Jesus, and her fingers grazed his clothing, her faith and courage paid off. She felt an instant healing. The years of uncertainty and suffering were gone. Gone!

Now it was Jesus's turn to take a risk. He could have ignored the incident, acted as if nothing had happened, and continued on his way. It was inappropriate to relate in public to a woman like her.

But it was not the way of the Savior to run from such encounters. Rather, it was his nature to reach out to those who had the smallest measure of faith. That is the full-life generous way.

"Who touched my clothes?" Jesus asked.

His disciples were incredulous that Jesus would ask this while the crowd flooded about him. You can hear them muttering, "*Who touched my clothes?* Jesus, really!" But the Lord was determined to engage with the healed woman so that he could send her on with a blessing.

Kneeling before him, she identified herself. Listen again to his words of blessing to her: "Go in peace; be freed from your suffering."

It is worth concentrating for a moment on just one detail in this story. A large crowd was wrestling for the Lord's attention, but only one person (a woman with some faith) connected with him. Is this the way of many religious gatherings? Do crowds gather out of curiosity, a quest for sensation? And is there just one, or a few, among the many who realize that the important thing is to touch the Lord and experience the power of his full-life generosity?

Ebenezer Asks: What would have happened to this woman if she had approached the disciples *first*? What marks of full-life generosity are modeled in the behavior of Jesus? What was his priority in this story?

Reflection: In this story, both Jesus and the woman took risks—the woman, by reaching out and touching Jesus, and Jesus, by addressing the woman and choosing to perform a miracle by healing her. How would you rank your ability to stretch yourself and take risks in your generosity and giving? Do you tend to be more cautious?

BeScrooged Activity: Would your spouse or friends call you an unhindered giver? Can you surprise someone today with your spontaneous and unconstrained generosity? Target one to three recipients.

DAY 13:
GRACE-DRIVEN GENEROSITY

READ LUKE 19:1-10

"When Jesus reached the spot, he looked up and said to him, 'Zacchaeus, come down immediately. I must stay at your house today.' So he came down at once and welcomed him gladly." (Luke 19:5)

WHO WAS ZACCHAEUS? WE KNOW HE WAS SHORT IN STATURE, and we know he was caught up in a highly corrupted profession as a collector of taxes and tolls. Also, we know he was universally despised. Perhaps his reputation was quite similar to that of the original Ebenezer Scrooge.

So why, when Jesus entered the village of Jericho, would he choose to visit with this offensive man, when he could have spent his time with the local synagogue president or the mayor? The answer to that question has everything to do with the notion of full-life generosity.

The two men, Jesus and Zacchaeus, began their encounter near a sycamore tree that Zacchaeus had climbed in order to get a better view of Jesus when he passed by. We can only guess what it was that caused the tax man to seek Jesus out.

Perhaps he had become convicted about the direction his life had taken. Perhaps he felt powerless to restart his life. Maybe he'd heard some stories about Jesus and his followers from Matthew, another tax collector, who'd undergone some kind of personal transformation.

What Zacchaeus could not know was that Jesus anticipated seeing him up in that tree. While the Lord had little time for those who refused to acknowledge their brokenness, he had plenty of time for those who knew they needed help. Apparently Zacchaeus was one of those.

Hence, Jesus's words when he reached the sycamore tree: "Come down; I must visit your house today."

The friends and critics of Jesus were furious when they saw Jesus head off in the company of this despicable man. The air must have been blue with criticism and accusation, but Jesus was scarcely intimidated.

What did Jesus and Zacchaeus talk about when they were alone? We don't know. But we can guess, based on their remarks when they returned to the waiting crowd.

Jesus: "Today salvation has come to this house, because this man, too, is a son of Abraham." Was he saying that Zacchaeus was now a man of faith? (Luke 19:9)

Zacchaeus (loosely translated): "I want to apologize for my greed and selfishness. I intend to restore what I've extorted to everyone I've hurt. I have a new life, and it will be marked by a fully-generous spirit." (Luke 19:8)

We can deduce from these words that Zacchaeus had come face to face with the generosity and grace of the Son of God. He was a changed man.

Jesus then spoke to those who remained confused about his intentions: "[I have] come to seek and to rescue lost people." (Luke 19:10) The words sound like a personal mission statement.

Ebenezer Asks: Why would Jesus prefer that his conversation with Zacchaeus be held in private? What is Jesus communicating by entering the home of a publically despised sinner? Who learns the most from this encounter?

Reflection: What kind of courage does it take to oppose the crowd's opinions and act on the basis of our personal convictions? How can we acquire this courage?

BeScrooged Activity: The gift of God's grace fuels our ability to be "grace-driven" generous people. Look for a few ways you can extend a "gesture of grace" today. Consider how Jesus always "led with love"—not judgment.

DAY 14:
WHEN GENEROSITY AND SELFISHNESS COLLIDE

READ LUKE 13:10-17

"On a Sabbath Jesus was teaching in one of the synagogues, and a woman was there who had been crippled by a spirit for eighteen years. She was bent over and could not straighten up at all. When Jesus saw her, he called her forward ..." (Luke 13:10-12)

ORGANIZED RELIGION HAS THE POTENTIAL TO SQUELCH THE SPIRIT of full-life generosity. This often occurs when a program or a tradition is allowed to control how we respond to the prompting of God's Spirit.

Here is a clear-cut example.

As rabbis often did on the Sabbath, Jesus guest-taught in a synagogue. In the audience was a woman who had been severely crippled (arthritis?) for eighteen years. Luke, the writer-physician, says, "She was bent over and could not straighten up at all."

At some point during his teaching, Jesus noticed her and invited her to come near. Without hesitation, he said, "Woman, you are set free from your infirmity." Instantly, she was able to stand straight. Her immediate response? Praise and thanksgiving to God!

But this story is not just about a woman freed to live in good health. It is also a story of how ugly things can become in the presence of the miserly.

The president of the synagogue objected to what Jesus had done, asserting that healings were forbidden on the Sabbath. Where could he have gotten such an idea? How could he not respond positively to what was clearly a work of God?

Occasionally we need to ask ourselves if we ever demonstrate the mentality of the synagogue president. It's possible this leader saw Jesus and his healing power as a threat to his own position. Perhaps he simply could not shake the traditional religious logic, which said there are certain things you don't do at certain times, even if it means the healing of a woman who has been crippled for eighteen years.

The Lord's rebuke of this man cut right to the heart of the matter. "You hypocrites!" he said. (Luke 13:115) This was not a moment for diplomacy. How, Jesus asked, could a man feel perfectly free to water his animals on the Sabbath, but not find acceptable the healing of someone who had suffered for years?

Jesus's argument was so airtight that the common people of the synagogue immediately broke into applause, while the president and his men slinked away in embarrassment. It was a triumphant moment for the gospel of full-life generosity.

Ebenezer Asks: What does the synagogue president's perspective teach us about a religious system that preaches a form of generosity, but lacks the will to practice what it preaches?

Reflection: Dig deep for the answer to this question. What perspectives live in me that might cause me to be jealous or critical of blessings offered to other people?

BeScrooged Activity: Celebrate and thank God for what you learned and were able to do this week. Share your experiences with someone else.

WHERE EBENEZER'S LADDER FINDS GENEROSITY

Ebenezer's Ladder has seven rungs, each representing an increasingly higher view of full-life generosity. Before looking at the final three rungs, let's quickly review the kind of people who stand on the first four.

At the bottom of the ladder, for example, there is the **consumer**, whose generosity emerges only after he has satisfied all his own wants and needs. In most cases this means that he or she exhibits very limited amounts of generosity.

On the next rung is the **deal-maker**, who's inspired to generosity only when he knows what he might get in return.

You'll find the **do-gooder** on the third rung. For him, generosity (whatever form it takes) is triggered only when he is awakened by a strong sense of excitement or dark feelings of guilt. What's missing in the life of a do-gooder? Deep belief, conviction, a certainty that God has created us to be full-life generous people. In short, the do-gooder acts generously only when his emotions are triggered.

The **cautious reflector** can be found on the fourth rung. He is driven by the need to feel secure. He may have grown up in poverty or been devastated in the past by a serious financial loss. So the thought of acting or giving generously is always prefaced by the question, "What is my risk factor here?" He ponders all the "what if" scenarios, such as loss of a job, a downturn in the economy, and the possibility of diminishing health. If he can rid himself of the fearfulness of the "what ifs," he might be willing—at least for the moment—to lean in the direction of full-life generosity.

What the people on the first four rungs of Ebenezer's Ladder need most is BeScroogement, an openness to Jesus's invitation to full-life generosity.

Writing to a small church of new Christians, St. Paul put it this way. "Be rooted (in your Christian life), be built up, be strengthened in faith you've been taught." And then he added this fourth thought: "be overflowing with thanksgiving." (Colossians 2:6-7)

This fourth idea, *overflowing with thanksgiving*, carries with it the idea of reciprocity in the Christian life. As we have received graciously from God, so should we respond with our own acts of generosity.

With that thought in mind we come the final three rungs on Ebenezer's Ladder. As we move toward the top of the ladder, we see with increasing clarity how full-life generosity looks. Each of these top three rungs requires an increasing sense of faith and trust in God, that he will never fail a generous person.

Please remember: none of us climbs Ebenezer's Ladder and remains on one rung. We will all have that occasional experience of going higher and then lower, lower and then higher. At this moment, the question we're asking is: on which rung do we stand today? And what would it take to climb a rung or two higher? Without realizing it, Ebenezer Scrooge went from the bottom of the ladder to the top in one night. One night! But, of course, Ebenezer's BeScroogement was fictional, and the spirits Marley sent in his direction were pretty forceful. It's possible they could cause BeScroogement in anyone.

The Seven Rungs of Ebenezer's Ladder

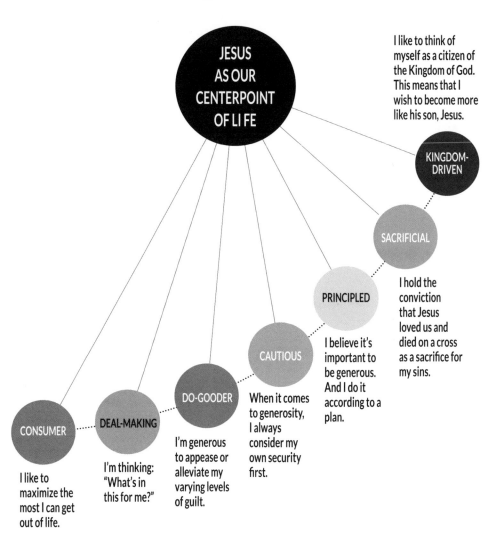

JESUS AS OUR CENTERPOINT OF LIFE

I like to think of myself as a citizen of the Kingdom of God. This means that I wish to become more like his son, Jesus.

KINGDOM-DRIVEN

SACRIFICIAL

PRINCIPLED

CAUTIOUS

DO-GOODER

DEAL-MAKING

CONSUMER

I hold the conviction that Jesus loved us and died on a cross as a sacrifice for my sins.

I believe it's important to be generous. And I do it according to a plan.

When it comes to generosity, I always consider my own security first.

I'm generous to appease or alleviate my varying levels of guilt.

I'm thinking: "What's in this for me?"

I like to maximize the most I can get out of life.

5. PRINCIPLED GENEROSITY

I really want to be known as a generous person. I believe it is important to be generous, and I make sure I'm faithful to living my life according to certain biblical principles. I want to serve God with the blessings I've received. What can/should I give back to God?

I've read enough books, heard enough sermons, and listened to enough people who sincerely believe that generosity is the way of the Christian. These principles have proven to me that the more consistently I follow them, the more I feel in alignment with God's ideals for my life.

My generosity tends to be tied to several areas of my "life plan" and how I believe I should live my life, be a strong follower of Christ, and steward my resources well.

I tend to be a planner in my life—and that instinct for planning applies to the way I look at generosity. While some people give in response to whatever arouses their feelings of compassion, I make my generosity decisions strategically and according to the way God leads me. I think God works this way in the lives of people like us.

Generosity is something I structure into my life. However, sometimes I wonder if it's almost too structured and that I am not looking for the spontaneous opportunities that God may be revealing to me. If there's a downside to my thinking, it's probably that I have become a bit too rigid, and it's possible that I don't listen to God enough when he calls upon me to stretch myself beyond the tithe on certain occasions.

I enjoy being in community with other Christians who believe and follow the same principles that I follow. We are better together when we are faithful and following God's intention for our lives.

6. SACRIFICIAL

I've been led more and more into a life of sacrificial living. It hasn't been an easy process, but it's been rewarding because I have started to discover the joy and true life God wants me to live. I have discovered that sacrificing more of my life and resources helps me understand what Jesus has done for me. This has resulted in a very intentional approach to my days.

I've learned to never regret my conscious decisions to resist materialistic society and all the traps that go along with those choices. I've come to know a powerful joy that results in living like this. In the largest sense it means saying a strategic "no" to myself so I can say "yes" to difference-making opportunities that God puts in my path. To put it another way, I've adopted a very popular slogan that is familiar to many: *It's not about me.*

Now, sacrificial generosity means there may be things I will never own, experiences I may never have, and places I may never go. Why? So I can be more responsive to the needs of others and serve God the way that he deserves to be glorified.

I'm naturally a very private person, and it's easy for me to withdraw into myself and make others take the first step in engaging me. But one day I sensed the voice of God saying I needed to make some changes in the way I approached people. I prayed for the courage and skill to invest in others and initiate encounters that resulted in encouragement and appreciation.

7. KINGDOM-DRIVEN

As a follower of Jesus Christ, I like to think of myself as a citizen of the 24/7 kingdom of God. I consciously listen for and invite the kingdom of God into my daily life and world.

This means I pray at the beginning of every day that Jesus will point me in the direction of people who need a friend: the aging, the child, the poor, the suffering. Whether I talk to them for one minute or for a few hours, I am on mission to meet them with the love of Jesus.

When I get to work each day, I ask God to help me work in such a way that others will experience of power of Christ. Part of generosity is making sure my employers get more from my contributions than the company has paid for. I try to do my work with purpose.

To me, generosity means praying for the world. When I read the newspapers or hear something about the world on TV, I try to respond to what I'm learning by praying for oppressed people, for nations where there is unspeakable suffering, for those who are desperately poor.

When it comes to material things, I have concluded that I actually own nothing, that God owns everything in my hands—so I try to treat the creation around me with care. I am sensitive to my small part of the world, to make sure I leave it as if Jesus might be the next person to come along. I want to properly manage everything entrusted to me (my body, my skills, my privileges, my material possessions) so everything reflects the goodness of Jesus.

The Bible says that someday God will greet those who have committed themselves to such kingdom generosity with gladness and affirmation. If it's possible, I want to be counted among them.

WEEK THREE

WE HAVE ALL HAD THE EXPERIENCE OF COMING UNDER THE THRALL of a highly persuasive speaker who convinces us to empty our pockets and provide funds for a compelling cause. We know what it's like to write a check after seeing the faces of frightened, hungry children barely surviving in squalid conditions. And we have felt the powerful urge that rises out of the depths of the soul when we hear of someone experiencing a catastrophic moment in life. This kind of generosity, though valid, is all too often incidental, impulsive, and emotional.

We seek a greater, a more substantial generosity (the kind we call full-life), which is rooted in the heart and which defines all of one's life. It's the kind of generosity that's demonstrated in the power of our personality and character, in the employment of our skills and capabilities, and in the wisdom of our experiences. This generosity is found in the depth of our feelings for people who are suffering and oppressed and in the strength we bring to a community of people who seek to care and support one another.

Where does such a broader concept of generosity come from? What are some of the biblical ideas that offer us a larger view of giving than many of us have ever realized previously? During this next week, we will reflect on seven propositions that flow from scripture and the culture of the Christian movement. It is in the power of these thoughts that we form our convictions about full-life generosity.

But first we return to Ebenezer Scrooge. What experiences brought about change in his life and transformed him into a generous giver? As he relates this part of his story, we see a three-step process that looked to the yesterdays of his life (what formed him), the today in his life (what he was refusing to face) and the tomorrows of his life (what would be his destiny if he did not change).

Scrooge had interesting questions to ponder.

"Suddenly, I knew I needed to change everything about myself. I needed a new way to live, to think, to use what I had for the benefit of people in my world. What was happening to me? I call it BeScroogement.

Called to Full-Life Generosity

Before he left, Marley told me I would be visited during the night by three spirits, or ghosts.

"Never! Not me! No way!" I responded.

But Marley did not accept my refusal.

"Take a hard look at me," he shouted. "If you resist these messengers and miss what they have to teach you, you're going to end up just like me—maybe worse. Are you hearing me?" Finally, he barked, "Be ready when the clock tolls one."

Then, Marley was gone. The building was deadly quiet and, numbed by fear and exhaustion, I fell into bed and was soon asleep.

Marley's three ghosts did come, one by one, just as he promised. The first introduced himself as the ghost of *Christmas Past*, the second the ghost of *Christmas Present*, and the third as the ghost of *Christmas Future*.

Each presented me with a picture of a part of my life I'd refused to face by myself. I am not exaggerating when I tell you that those three ghosts penetrated to the center of my soul. And when they were finished with me that night, all I could do was cry for mercy. Suddenly, I knew I needed to change everything about myself. I needed a new way to live, to think, to use what I had for the benefit of people in my world. What was happening to me? I call it *BeScroogement*.

Let me walk you through that unbelievable, life-changing night.

Christmas Past

The Ghost of Christmas Past escorted me back to my youngest years. We actually flew, if you can imagine it, and as we soared across the land of my childhood, I began to recognize people and places I'd not seen for a long time.

"I know this country like the back of my hand," I said to the ghost as I felt a sudden rise of emotion. "I could make my way around these parts blindfolded."

Suddenly, we stopped at the door of the boarding school to which my father had sent me when I was a small boy. This school held no pleasant memories for me at all. Nevertheless, the ghost insisted I go inside and look about. Soon I saw a vision of myself as a boy, alone in a room with a book. A flood of painful memories—abandonment, loneliness, fear—were unleashed in my heart. I'd spent years stuffing these memories deep within myself. And now, in the wink of an eye, they were all back. Had they ever really left me?

Then a young girl entered the room. My sister!

She hugged and kissed me and said, "My dear brother. I've come to take you back home. Did you hear me? You're leaving this place. You're coming home."

For reasons unexplained, my father's attitude toward me had changed, and he'd sent my sister to fetch me. He wanted me back—my father wanted me to come home.

"Our father is a different man now," my sister said. "He's kind and affectionate. Our home has become a heavenly place."

I soon learned that my sister was right.

But, despite my father's change of heart, I don't think I ever got over the pain of his sending me away. Perhaps that was the beginning of my determination never to fall under anyone's control again. Perhaps that's why wealth became my idol. With money, I must have reasoned, I could be totally independent.

A few years later my beloved sister died after giving birth to a son. Before she died, she named the baby Fred. Yes, that baby is the same Fred who invades my office every Christmas Eve to invite me to his home for dinner.

Soon the Ghost of Christmas Past and I were on to other places.

We stopped at a familiar business establishment owned by the man who had given me my first job. He was still there. His name was Fezziwig.

"It's Fezziwig!" I cried out when I saw him. "What a man Fezziwig was!"

Seeing this man reminded me of something I'd forgotten: Fezziwig had been an incredibly big-hearted man, the perfect example of full-life generosity.

"Fezziwig knew just how to make people feel significant and cared for," I said to the ghost. "He worked hard to make his business a happy place for his employees. He was a great encourager. He … he believed in me. And now that I see him again, I realize how much I must have disappointed him when I left to do other things."

Again the scene shifted. Suddenly, the ghost and I were overhearing a conversation I'd had long ago with Alice, a brilliant, beautiful young woman whom I'd loved and planned to marry. She wore a tiny ring I'd given her in anticipation of a future wedding. At the time it was all I could afford.

As I listened, I heard Alice repeat words that have haunted me all these years. "Ebenezer, an idol has replaced me in your life. And I can see that it's making you happier than I've been able to."

"What are you saying?" I asked her. "What idol are you talking about?"

"A golden one," she answered.

I recalled again how Alice had become increasingly sensitive to my ambition to become a wealthy man.

"There is nothing I fear more than poverty," I heard myself reason with Alice. "And there is nothing that offers greater security than success and wealth." Pause for a moment, reader, and consider these words.

"You worry too much about wealth," Alice returned. "It's eroding your character and your convictions. You're becoming a possessed man."

"But I love you," I pleaded.

Alice shook her head. "When you and I became engaged we were both poor, and we were content. We worked hard; we had dreams and visions about a wonderful, happy future. But things have changed, Ebenezer. You're no longer the man you used to be, the man I once loved."

"But I was so young then. Back then I didn't understand—"

"Back then, Ebenezer, you and I were one-hearted. But now that connection's gone. I need for you to know that I have given this a lot of thought, and I've decided to release you from our commitment. I hope you're satisfied with the way of life you have now chosen. It's a life that doesn't include me."

As the ghost and I listened to this conversation that had taken place so many years ago, I wanted to cry out, "Alice, you were right! I made the wrong choice. I'll change!" But the words stuck in my throat.

Alice and I never saw each other again after that conversation. Now I am beginning to understand how perceptive she was. That golden idol, as she called it, did turn into an addiction, a captivity. I was soon beyond anyone's help. Even the sound of my name—Scrooge—somehow described the kind of man I had become.

✟✟✟

The Ghost of Christmas Past had one more place he wished to take me. It was the living room of a house I'd never seen before. A man and his wife—I didn't recognize either of them—were talking. I heard the husband say, "I saw an old friend of yours this afternoon, my dear. Mr. Scrooge."

"Where did you see him?" his wife asked.

"I was walking by the offices of Scrooge and Marley and looked in the window. There was Scrooge sitting alone at his desk. Only a candle lit the room. Later, I heard that his business partner, Jacob Marley, is dying. Imagine it. The only thing the man can think to do is work."

Then I suddenly realized what I was seeing. This man who'd passed by my office window was Alice's husband, the man she married instead of me.

Soon afterward, the Ghost of Christmas Past disappeared.

Christmas Present

When the bell of the clock tolled again that night, I was better prepared. The second of Marley's promised ghosts—Christmas Present—appeared, and I said to him, "Spirit, take me where you want. I am prepared for anything you have to teach me. I have much learning to do."

Recalling those words now ("take me where you want"), it occurs to me that BeScroogement was already beginning its work in my heart. For the first time in my life, I was opening myself up to acknowledge the kind of man I'd become. Yes, it was humbling. Yes, it hurt. But this was exactly what needed to happen if I was ever to become a fully-generous man.

Under the guidance of the Ghost of Christmas Present, I soon found myself—invisible, of course—in the home of Bob Cratchit and his family. As I remarked earlier, I had never been there before.

Bob and his youngest son, Tim, a severely disabled child, had just arrived home from Christmas worship at church. I had known nothing about this boy until that moment. I guess I chose not to know because that might have pushed me into feelings of compassion, obligation, and responsibility. And you know where that leads: full-life generosity.

But now that I was in the Cratchit home, I became curious. "Spirit," I whispered nervously, "does this boy have a long life ahead of him?"

"See that empty chair off in the corner?" the ghost pointed. "That's his, and when I look into the future, I don't see anyone sitting in it any longer. So, I'll be honest with you. If nothing changes, it looks to me as if the boy will die."

"No, merciful Spirit," I blurted out. "Can't you say that he will live?"

"I can't. It's this simple. If there is no medical treatment—and the family cannot afford such treatment—this will be his last Christmas. But why should that bother you, anyway? If the boy dies, the surplus population of the world will be thinned out just a bit. Isn't that how you put it a few hours ago to the two men from the neighborhood charity who paid you a visit?"

The Ghost of Christmas Present had used my own words to rebuke me. I was shocked when I heard them spoken back to me.

"Perhaps," the ghost went on, "you should think more before you speak. How would you feel if Heaven declared that you were a part of the so-called surplus population, that you were to be eliminated?"

Conversation over!

Before we left the Cratchit home, I studied the family once more. The Cratchits might have been terribly poor, but it was clear that they were content, thankful, and at peace with the world and with one another.

I found myself thinking, "I'd give anything to be a part of this family." The Cratchits were what a full-life generous family looks like.

As we left the Cratchit home, I looked back for a final glimpse of Tiny Tim. Just looking at him awakened in me a feeling I thought I'd lost many years ago: love.

The Ghost of Christmas Present next took me to the home of my nephew, Fred. For how many years had I been resisting his invitation to visit? Now, the choice was no longer mine to make.

Approaching the house, I overheard Fred and his family in the midst of conversation. They were talking about me.

"Uncle Scrooge called Christmas, 'humbug'! He really believes that!" Fred was saying as he laughed. "He's getting old, not as pleasant as he could be, but I won't be his judge. I'm sure he's very rich, but of what use is the wealth? He does next to nothing with it. He doesn't spend it on himself. And he certainly doesn't use it for the betterment of anyone else. And I can tell you this: we'll never see any of it."

"I want nothing to do with him," Fred's wife said sharply.

"Oh, I do. Actually, I feel very badly for him," Fred replied. "I couldn't get angry with him if I tried. He's his own worst enemy. He won't come and dine with us, for example. That's his loss. He misses out on a great dinner, and he misses out on a family that might love him. An old man needs both."

Fred went on. "I'll keep on inviting him to our home every year, whether he likes it or not, and he'll probably rage at me until the day he dies. But I'm going back every year to say, 'Uncle, how are you?' If the only thing I accomplish is to convince him to leave his poor clerk, Cratchit, a small inheritance, I'll have accomplished something."

I have to say it again. Fred, this nephew of mine, is a full-life generous man.

The ghost and I made several other stops. We visited hospitals, prisons, and shelters for the homeless. But despite the almost-universal poverty and the suffering in those places, we saw people eating, worshipping, and presenting gifts to one another.

I was left to ask myself: *Am I the only man in this world who doesn't love Christmas?*

My time with the Ghost of Christmas Present was about to end. But before it did, he had one final, terribly upsetting message for me.

I happened to notice something moving inside his robe. I pointed to it.

The ghost parted his robe, and there I saw two small children, a boy and a girl. Both were malnourished, diseased, and snarling with anger.

"Are they yours?" I asked.

"They are every man's," the ghost responded. "The boy's name is *Ignorance*; the girl's *Need*. Scrooge, you neglect them at your peril. If you do neglect them, and if you ignore those who speak on their behalf, you will suffer terrible consequences. You will find them in the streets doing unspeakable things."

"What are you suggesting? What can we do for them?" I asked.

"Are there no prisons?" he replied. "Are there no workhouses? Did you not also speak those words just a few hours ago?"

Again, the ghost left me to form my own conclusions.

Christmas Future

Marley's third ghost was tall, stately, and utterly silent. He merely pointed in whatever direction he willed for us to go.

"Am I in the presence of the Ghost of Christmas Future?" I asked.

The ghost said nothing.

"I worry about you more than the others who have come to me," I said anxiously. "But since I know your intention is to do me good, and since I know I'm in need of heart-change, I am ready to listen and learn with an accepting heart."

The spirit beckoned to me, and immediately we were transported to another part of the city, to a marketplace that was thoroughly familiar. A madness was in the air as crowds of people swarmed about. Currencies of all denominations passed from hand to hand. Here and there were groups loudly negotiating contracts. Merchants were haggling with customers over the cost of goods. Everyone kept looking impatiently at their watches because they had more appointments, more deals to make.

It occurred to me that this circus of people was not a place where one could speak about the greater issues of life. There was no dignity here, no compassion, no inquiry into the welfare of others. The only thing that drew people to this place was that golden idol called money. They were here to get their piece of it. I knew the crowd well; I had often been a part of it.

After I'd had the chance to take it all in, the Ghost pointed to one little knot of businessmen. We moved closer to hear what they were saying.

"No, I haven't heard the details," said one. "Just that he's dead."

"So, how did he die?" asked another.

"Only God knows," replied the first, yawning.

"What's going to happen to his money?"

"I haven't heard. Maybe his company will get it. All I know is that I'm not in the will."

"I suspect it will be a very inexpensive funeral. Who will go to it? Do you think we should get some people together and make a showing?"

"I'll go if they serve food." Everyone laughed.

At first, I was confused. Were they talking about Marley? Certainly not him. He'd been gone for seven years. No one else came to mind.

And then came the devastating realization that *they were speaking about me.*

The ghost escorted me toward another part of the city, a part I'd never visited before. I saw several people fighting over someone's personal effects.

"He should have been a more decent person," a woman was saying. "If he had treated people with just a smidgen of kindness, he'd have had somebody to look after him when he died instead of dying alone."

Was I the man who lacked decency? Was I the one who'd died alone?

I must confess to you. There was an almost unbearable pain growing in my soul. BeScroogement can be a terrible experience if you've spent as many years hardening your heart as I have.

Yet there was more that the ghost of Christmas Future wanted me to see.

We were suddenly in a bedroom. I felt a fresh sense of dread creeping over me. On the bed a filthy sheet covered a human shape. I knew I was supposed to lift the sheet to see who was there, but I drew back. I was fairly certain what I'd see.

"Spirit," I said, "I can't stand this awful place. I get the message. Trust me! I have to get out of here!"

The ghost extended his dark robe, and instantly we were back in Bob Cratchit's home. You won't be surprised that the first thing I looked for was Tiny Tim. But now he was missing. I needed no one to tell me Tiny Tim was dying. When I looked at the faces of Bob and his wife, I was shaken by the grief I saw. I began to ask myself: *What can I do to save this boy's life?*

Soon the ghost led me away from that sad home and to a church graveyard that was dark and neglected. I cannot exaggerate the dreariness of the place. We walked silently among the graves until the ghost pointed to one and motioned me toward it. I stiffened because I was sure I knew whose name was on the face of that stone.

Once again I wanted to leave that place, but this time the ghost would not let me off the hook.

"Before I approach the stone," I said, "can you tell me one thing? Have we been observing things that *will* be or things that *could* be?"

The ghost remained silent.

I lost whatever composure I had left, and I shouted at him. "The way a man lives offers an idea of where he will end up—so if he changes his ways, if he repents, won't the future turn out differently? Please, please tell me that a change of life is possible, that I can be BeScrooged!"

Still, the ghost did not respond.

Finally, I edged close enough to read the words on the gravestone. There I saw what I already knew I would see: my miserable-sounding name, EBENEZER SCROOGE.

"Why do I have to see this," I shouted once again, "if my life cannot be changed?"

And in that moment I saw the complete truth about myself. I realized I must renounce the selfish man I'd become and declare my intention to commit to full-life generosity.

"I will honor Christmas in my heart," I cried, "and I will try to keep Christmas throughout all the year. I will live in the past, the present, and the future. The spirits of all three shall continually work within me. I will not resist the lessons that they teach."

"Please, tell me," I shouted at the ghost, "may I erase the name on this stone?"

The Ghost of Christmas Future appeared to tremble at my question. Then he seemed to collapse, and he merged with the post at the foot of my bed.

Instantly, I awakened and realized I was under the covers in my own bed. I also sensed that I was a different man than the one who had crawled into bed hours before. Something in me had indeed changed. I had become *BeScrooged*.

DAY 15:
WHY SHOULD WE LIVE GENEROUSLY?

BECAUSE WE HAVE A GENEROUS GOD WHO CREATES AND GIVES OUT OF HIS GRACE

"In the beginning God created the heavens and the earth." (Genesis 1:1)

"By faith we understand that the universe was formed at God's command, so that what is seen was not made out of what was visible." (Hebrews 11:3)

"What is man that you are mindful of him, the son of man that you care for him?" (Psalm 8:4)

ONCE THERE WAS NOTHING. AND THEN GOD SPOKE. "Let there be…," he said, and in a mysterious sequence of events an infinite and beautiful universe sprang into being. This was the very first act of generosity.

What God created was not produced out of old or recycled material. "The universe," the New Testament writer says, "was formed by God's command."

What God created, he blessed. To bless means that one stamps value on what he intends to give. Strange as it may sound, nothing has value until it is blessed by the one who made it. When an artist signs his work, for example, he is saying that the piece is finished and that it reveals his fullest intentions. And so it was that God carefully blessed everything he made. Put simply, he signed his work!

God's creation included more than galaxies, planets, mountains, and oceans. God created people and placed them in the middle of his artwork.

These would be people who could appreciate beauty, express joy, invent things, think, love one another, and work together. Having brought such people into being, God gave his creation to them and charged them to explore, to enjoy, and to manage it.

A child comes home from school with a gift. It is a piece of handmade jewelry, a bracelet the child has made for her mother. The bracelet is roughly shaped and not that attractive. Its surfaces are daubed with clashing paints. No one would pick it out in a jewelry store.

But the bracelet's imperfections and gaudiness are no matter. The mother receives the gift with gladness. She will wear it proudly.

Why? Because her daughter made it and gave it to her. It speaks of the generosity of time and effort. It is the daughter's way of saying to her mom, "I love you."

God's gift of creation was neither fragile nor crudely shaped. Yet it too conveys a message. God says, creation is a gift that reveals my character and my love. It is yours to enjoy, yours to discover, yours to use if you use it respectfully and thankfully.

Ebenezer Asks: If God is generous in all that he does, how should we respond to him? How will our response affect our day-to-day priorities?

Reflection: What are your thoughts concerning the way people treat God's creation? Is creation seen as a gift? Do people regard it with a thankful spirit?

BeScrooged Activity: If you know of a place in your community that has been despoiled and badly littered, consider going there today and doing something that might restore a part of it to its intended attractiveness.

Also, try making a list of things you often ignore or take for granted: things that sustain health and life, things that are beautiful, things that elevate our quality of life. Read your list to friends or family and express your appreciation.

DAY 16:
WHY SHOULD WE LIVE GENEROUSLY?

BECAUSE GENEROSITY OFFERS US A WAY TO EXPRESS OUR WORSHIP AND THANKFULNESS TO GOD

"When you have entered the land the Lord your God is giving you as an inheritance and have taken possession of it and settled in it, take some of the first fruits of all that you produce from the soil of the land the Lord your God is giving you and put them in a basket. Then go to the place the Lord your God will choose as a dwelling for his name and say to the priest in office at the time, "I declare today to the Lord your God that I have come to the land the Lord swore to our forefather to give us...Place the basket before the Lord your God and bow down before him." (Deuteronomy 26:1-15)

OUT OF ABRAHAM'S FAMILY LINE CAME THE NATION OF ISRAEL, the people of God. The formation of Israel did not come swiftly or easily. There was, for example, a four hundred-year period in Egypt when the people were exploited as slaves by the Egyptians. During that time, they owned nothing, had no power, and found it hard to conceive of any kind of future. In short, they were stripped of their dignity.

Then Moses appeared. God had groomed him for eighty years to be Israel's liberating leader. Eighty years! His first task was to face down the Egyptian pharaoh and gain the freedom of his people. With God's help he succeeded. And so the day came when the

Hebrew people exited Egypt, journeyed into the desert, and headed for the Promised Land. Because they were an undisciplined, almost faithless people, what could have been a reasonably brief journey lasted for forty years.

But the forty years, while often miserable, were not wasted. It became a time of learning, of deepening, of growing into God's ways. It fell to Moses to teach the people—these ex-slaves—how to organize themselves socially and spiritually.

Among the very first things that Moses taught them was the principle of the Sabbath. God's people were to allocate one day a week for worship and rest. On that day everything came to a stop.

Then came the issue of generosity. A people seeking to form a community must learn the meaning and use of wealth. How will it be generated? How will it be used? And how will the people make sure that wealth does not capture and control their hearts?

The answer lies in the principle of the first fruits.

As long as the Israelites traveled in the desert, they could anticipate God's care for them. When they feared that they might go hungry, for example, God provided them a daily portion of manna. The lesson? If they trusted God, they would never be without.

When they reached the Promised Land, the Hebrews would be in a position to produce "plenty." The new land would be fertile, the wells deep, the trees fruitful, and the pastures verdant.

But if Israel was to receive this gift of the Promised Land from God, the people had to acquire an understanding of the full-life generous spirit. With blessing comes responsibility. *Israel had to learn how to give.* Thus, the principle of the first fruits. This principle provided the foundation for an understanding of full-life generosity.

As a starting discipline, each family was asked to gather ten percent (a tithe) of the first, the best, the most perfect of the results of their work—grain, fruit, animals—and bring it to the altar. Does it need to be said that the first fruits were *never* damaged, throw-away goods?

Generous giving, Israel learned, meant quantity *and* quality.

When presenting their gifts to the priest, the people were instructed to say, "Now I bring the first fruits of the soil that you, O Lord, have given to me" (Deuteronomy 26:10). Saying this on every occasion reminded the giver that he was acting generously because God had been generous first.

The gifts people brought provided for the maintenance of the worship center (the tabernacle), for the poor, for the widows and orphans, for the alien and the stranger. In this way, the people of God learned a most important lesson: giving, and giving generously, was indispensable to genuine faith.

Ebenezer asks: One of the first things Moses taught Israel was the law of the first fruits: how to give generously. What is the implication for Christians today? If we choose to be biblically guided in life, then what must be our attitude toward full-life generosity?

Reflection: What were the circumstances under which you first learned how to give? Who introduced the idea to you in your earliest years? How easily did you adopt giving as part of your way of life?

BeScrooged Activity: What do the concepts of "first fruits" (quality) and tithe (quantity) mean to you? Do you have any such standards in your giving disciplines? If you do not, consider giving an experimental percentage of income that will stretch you for four weeks. Do this with the anticipation that God will touch your life in some extraordinary way during the course of this full-life generosity exercise.

DAY 17:
WHY SHOULD WE LIVE GENEROUSLY?

BECAUSE WE FOLLOW JESUS, WHO PERSONIFIED FULL-LIFE GENEROSITY BY ASSUMING THE ROLE OF A SERVANT IN ALL HE DID AND BY SACRIFICING HIS LIFE FOR US

"In everything I did, I showed you that by this kind of hard work, we must help the weak, remembering the words the Lord Jesus himself said, 'It is more blessed to give than to receive.'" (Acts 20:35)

"He came to that which was his own, but his own did not receive him. Yet to those who received him, to those who believed in his name, he gave the right to become children of God." (John 1:11)

"Greater love has no one than this, that he lay down his life for his friends. You are my friends." (John 15:13)

THERE IS HARDLY A STORY IN THE LIFE OF JESUS THAT DOES NOT PICTURE HIM expressing some dimension of generous living. Jesus was always seeking to be a giver, not a taker. For the sick, there was healing. For the blind, there was sight. For a broken man crazed by inner demons, there was a return to wholeness. For the disabled, there were new limbs. For the hungry, there was bread. And for a grieving mother, there was the resurrection of a son who had succumbed to death.

Jesus gave time to children, gave honor to women who were ordinarily devalued, gave dignity to those who were old and discarded, and kept company with the poor.

To his disciples, he opened his heart and gave them, as he put it, the secrets of the kingdom. One of those secrets was that we were not originally created to be selfish, but that we were "wired" to be givers—generous givers. When the disciples failed miserably (Simon Peter comes to mind), Jesus reached out and offered second, third, and fourth chances. He gave straight answers to their questions, showed patience when they went off on tangents, and affirmed them when they did something right.

In the end, in the supreme moment, Jesus gave his life at the cross so all who had faith in him would receive the gift of eternal life.

All these things and many more actions of full-life generosity leave us with a strong message. The more one desires to emulate the character and the spirit of Jesus Christ, the more generous he becomes. What Jesus is saying to us by way of example is that generous giving is not only about money. It is about all the dimensions of one's life. As a new, slightly irreverent follower of Jesus once said after studying the public work of the Lord, "He was one powerful giving machine."

A giving machine? This is a rather strange way of describing the ways of the Son of God. But it clearly suggests that the speaker understands Jesus's heart and mission.

Ebenezer Asks (candidly): What story from the life of Jesus provokes you in terms of understanding the power of full-life generosity?

Reflection: Review the categories of people in this meditation that Jesus is said to have touched. Which of these groups gains your attention most naturally?

BeScrooged Activity: Ask God to bring to your mind three people with whom you are acquainted who are in some form of difficulty. Write them a note of encouragement and assure them of your prayers and concern.

The generous life of Christ teaches us how to be proactive givers rather than takers. Today, ask God to put you in a position where you can be more intentional and creative about being a generous giver to someone.

DAY 18:
WHY SHOULD WE LIVE GENEROUSLY?

BECAUSE WE ARE FILLED WITH THE HOLY SPIRIT, WHO SEEKS TO CHANGE US INTO GENEROUS PEOPLE

"Our gospel came to you not simply with words, but also with the power of the Holy Spirit and with deep conviction…You welcomed the message with joy given by the Holy Spirit." (I Thessalonians 1:5-6)

"The Counselor, the Holy Spirit, whom the Father will send in my name, will teach you all things and will remind you of everything I have said to you." (John 14:25)

"When the Spirit of truth comes, he will guide you into all truth." (John 16:13)

"You will receive power when the Holy Spirit comes on you; and you will be my witnesses…" (Acts 1:8)

THE HOLY SPIRIT—THE THIRD MEMBER OF THE TRINITY—is the full-life generous gift of Jesus to his followers. If Jesus is going to return to his Father in heaven, then it is the Holy Spirit's task to act in his place, giving strength and reinforcing truth for those who will spread Jesus's gospel across the world. Just as the Father and Son give, so the Holy Spirit comes to give. Give what?

He gives people confidence that they are truly adopted as the sons and daughters of

Jesus.

He makes the words and the lessons of Jesus come alive and become relevant in the lives of those in the believing community.

He empowers the people of the new Christian movement to be bold, loving, and forthright in how they represent the gospel.

He gives capabilities and skills—called gifts—to the people of the Christian way so all members of the family of God can be participants in the work of the Lord.

He convicts and prods those who are in danger of straying from the faith.

He gives insight to those who are listening for the voice of God.

Finally, he amplifies the power of our prayers so they reach heaven with force.

"Be filled with the Holy Spirit," Paul wrote to the Ephesians (Ephesians 5:18). And then he added further encouragements about the way they should speak to each other, sing together, give thanks, and serve one another. All these are evidence of a new way, a generous way, of living.

All this comes courtesy of the Holy Spirit, whose generosity makes the church possible.

Ebenezer asks: How might our generosity excel when we "tap into" the voice and direction of the Holy Spirit in our lives?

Reflection: What strengths or abilities do you have that you believe are a gift from the Holy Spirit? Do you use them only to enhance your own interests, or are you aware that you use them for the blessing of others? What role has the Holy Spirit played in your life to encourage your generosity?

BeScrooged Activity: This would be a good day to pray and ask the Holy Spirit to reveal how your unique giftedness can be used to encourage your generosity.

DAY 19:
WHY SHOULD WE LIVE GENEROUSLY?

BECAUSE WE ARE TAUGHT BY THE PRECEDENT OF THE FIRST CHRISTIANS, WHO WERE SELFLESSLY, SACRIFICIALLY, AND REDEMPTIVELY GENEROUS TO ONE ANOTHER

"All the believers were together and had everything in common. Selling their possessions and goods, they gave to anyone as he had need." (Acts 2:44)

"All the believers were one in heart and mind. No one claimed that any of their possessions was their own, but they shared everything they had… And God's grace was so powerfully at work in them all that there were no needy persons among them. For from time to time those who owned land or houses sold them, brought the money from the sales and put it at the apostles' feet, and it was distributed to anyone who had need." (Acts 4:32-35)

"Whoever sows sparingly will reap sparingly, and whoever sows generously will reap generously. Each man should give what he has decided in his heart to give, not reluctantly or under compulsion, but God loves a cheerful giver." (II Corinthians 9:8)

THE BRAND-NEW JERUSALEM CONGREGATION described in the early chapters of Acts offers a vivid description of generosity gone viral. Most of the fledgling Christians had little personal history with any act of generosity—giving money, serving others, caring for the weak—at all. If they gave in the past, it was usually under duress and obligation. But full-life generosity? Unlikely!

In this new movement, a different kind of giver appeared. This giver was one who had been transformed by the gospel of Jesus Christ. The primary evidence of their transformation was a powerful sensitivity to others. A quick and joyful response to human need.

"No one claimed that any of their possessions was their own," the writer of the book of Acts says. This is his way of saying that these new Christians had experienced a radical change of heart about caring for one another and sharing their material things. They were convinced that their possessions and resources needed to be shared with those who had nothing. The outcome? "There were no needy persons among them," the book of Acts says.

Many Christians became—as Paul describes the Thessalonians—cheerful, enthusiastic givers. Generosity was at the root of their conversion. Thus they had no need for anyone to beg them to give abundantly. It's quite possible that they would have been unresponsive to the methods of persuasion that are used today to plead with people to be generous. These first Christians cared for the sick, offered hospitality to the widows and the orphans, and fed those who were hungry or who could not take care of themselves—because that was what they understood Christ-following to be about.

In a loveless culture where most people had their minds only on themselves, the Christian reputation for love and generosity grabbed the attention and admiration of people everywhere.

Ebenezer Asks: What would it be like to be part of a gathering of Christ-followers (like these early Christians) whose core purpose was to intentionally live out the generous gospel and care for all the needy in a given community?

Reflection: How does the generosity of the earliest Acts church differ from the "generosity" of people in the modern Christian movement?

BeScrooged Activity: As we embody the generous nature of God and become his "hands and feet" in the world, consider these following ideas as ways to enhance your day-to-day full-life generosity. Write down a few tangible ways that each of these can become an intentional and consistent part of your generous story. How can you deepen these in your life? Use the Acts Church as your guide!

- Deepen your passion to become a reflection of the gospel and life of Jesus by being a brighter beacon of light, hope, and compassion to others.
- Deepen your passion for advocating for unjust and inhumane issues by pursuing greater "generous justice" and human kindness.
- Deepen your passion for helping the suffering, hungry, and broken people in the world.

DAY 20:
WHY SHOULD WE LIVE GENEROUSLY?

BECAUSE WE ARE INFLUENCED BY SEVERAL CENTURIES OF CHRISTIANS WHOSE GOSPEL MESSAGE TO THE WORLD WAS AUTHENTICATED BY FULL-LIFE GENEROSITY

Tertullian (160-220 AD): "It is our care for the helpless, our practice of loving kindness, that brands us in the eyes of many of our opponents. 'Only look,' they say, 'look how they love one another...Look how they are prepared to die for one another.'"

Dionysius (250 AD): "[The pagans] thrust aside anyone who began to be sick and kept aloof even from their dearest friends, and cast the sufferers out upon the public roads half dead...very many of our [Christian] brethren, while in their exceeding love and brotherly kindness, did not spare themselves, but kept by each other and visited the sick without thought of their own peril..."

Eusebius of Caesarea (263-339 AD): "For the Christians were the only people who amidst such terrible ills showed their fellow feelings and humanity by their actions. Day by day some would busy themselves with attending the dead and burying them...others gathered in one spot all who were afflicted by hunger...and gave bread to them all. When this became known, people glorified the Christian God and, convinced by the very facts, confessed that the Christians alone were truly pious and religious."

A FRIEND WHO IS AN ANTHROPOLOGIST ONCE SAID TO ME that the culture of a village or city (or any group, for that matter) cannot be fully understood until its "economic component" is described. Its *economic component*? We're talking about the process by which any community of people creates wealth, accumulates it, uses it, and disposes of it. Until all this is understood, the culture cannot be fully understood.

It is interesting to note that the early Christian community was very much aware of the economic component in its life together. When the Church fathers began to describe the uniqueness of the Christian community, they were quick to note how much full-life generosity was a part of it.

In his book *The Rise of Christianity*, Rodney Stark is very certain that the authenticating mark of the Christian faith was found in the way Christians chose to be generous to friends and enemies in the name of Jesus. He writes: "Pagan and Christian writers are unanimous not only that Christian Scripture stressed love and charity as the central duties of faith, *but that these were sustained in everyday behavior*." (italics ours)

Stark and other scholars take a hard look at the three centuries after Christ and see an accumulation of disasters that overtook one city of the Roman empire after another. Plagues, fire, earthquakes, and military conquests all took a terrible toll on local populations.

The response of Pagans to these disasters was mostly to run, to protect themselves, and to ignore the plight of those who were suffering. But the response of Christians? To stay behind and nurse the sick, dispose of the dead, feed the hungry, and take in the orphan. Full-life generosity.

No wonder the Christian movement expanded, Stark says. If one's life had been spared through the efforts of people who practiced love and generosity, wouldn't he want to join them?

The important thing to take away from this moment in history is the realization that early Christians offered the world far more than just words. They offered a daily compassion that was full-life generous. Do Christians still do this today?

Ebenezer Asks: How well do you think your church practices full-life generosity? What evidence can you point to? Or, what concerns do you have?

Reflection: Tertullian says the love Christians had for one another was obvious to the pagans who observed them. Could this be said of the Christian community today?

BeScrooged Activity: Visit a local public school and ask the head administrator if there is one thing their students need and cannot afford. Organize a group of Christians and find a way to provide for that need. Some examples: backpacks, hats and gloves, shoes, medical treatment. What about food for the weekends? Statistics show that impoverished kids often go hungry when they are not at school. Donations for gently used clothing for struggling families can also be a great gift.

DAY 21:
WHY SHOULD WE LIVE GENEROUSLY?

BECAUSE WE KNOW THAT ONE DAY WE WILL BE HELD ACCOUNTABLE FOR WHAT WE HAVE DONE WITH WHAT WE HAVE BEEN GIVEN

"All the nations will be gathered before him, and he will separate the people one from another as a shepherd separates the sheep from the goats...The king will say to those on his right, 'Come, take your inheritance, the kingdom prepared for you since the creation of the world. For I was hungry, and you gave me something to eat. I was thirsty and you gave me something to drink. I was a stranger, and you invited me in. I needed clothes and you clothed me. I was sick and you looked after me. I was in prison and you came to visit me." (Matthew 25:31-40)

THIS IS A TROUBLESOME SCRIPTURE FOR ANYONE WHO IS UNCOMFORTABLE with the notion that we must all appear before God someday and account for our full-life generosity, or our lack of it.

In a parable that is enormous in scope, the Lord—seated on a throne—divides the people of the nations into two groups as a shepherd might separate his sheep from his goats.

For those to his right, the sheep, there is a *blessing*, the gift of a special place in the eternal kingdom of God, which has been prepared since the first days of creation. For those on his left, the goats, there is *judgment*. And what were the criteria used to make the separation that led to blessing or judgment? The practice of full-life generosity.

Further in the story the King identifies six forms of human suffering: hunger, thirst, lack of shelter, lack of clothing, sickness, and imprisonment. What was necessary to alleviate this suffering? Food, drink, hospitality, clothing, care, and visitation. Perhaps the six forms of suffering are meant to represent a greater cluster of human needs. And perhaps the six kinds of giving are meant to illustrate ways in which God's people are called upon to give.

Obviously those on the right—the sheep—had responded to these human needs magnificently. In fact they did it so instinctively, so cheerfully, they'd forgotten when they had given or who had received their gifts.

They asked the King, "*When* did we see you hungry, thirsty, homeless, naked, sick, and imprisoned?"

His answer? Every time you provided generously for those in your pathway who were in trouble, you were giving generously to me. What an amazing surprise!

But the story does not end well. Those on the left—the goats—are confounded. They might have acted differently had they been aware that Jesus was mysteriously present in all these generous exchanges. But they were not aware. Having paid no attention to the destitute, they are said to have paid no attention to Christ.

The underlying message of this story commands our attention. How many times each day have we passed by the victims of our communities and ignored them? How often have we been distracted by other things we thought more important? Were we ignoring Christ?

Ebenezer Asks: How do you respond to the King's comment, "Every time you provided for those who were in trouble, you were giving generously to me?"

Reflection: Think back on the last few days. Can you remember times when you resisted the impulse (or the leading of the Holy Spirit) to act generously? What are the things that may distract you from being generous?

BeScrooged Activity: Invite someone you might ordinarily avoid to meet you for lunch or coffee. This could be someone where you work, where you worship, or where you go to school. What kind of encouragement can you offer? What questions can you ask to get to know this person better? Think about your words deliberately beforehand.

THE WAFTS & WEAVES OF GENEROSITY

The creation of tapestries is an ancient craft. It is the work of artisans who skillfully interlace threads—cotton, wool, linen, or silk, for example—and create a durable, carpet-like fabric.

Tapestries have a broad range of usefulness. Some can be found on the walls of museums. Others cover floors in castles, mansions, cathedrals, or palaces.

A weaver may build an unusual abstract design into his tapestry. Or, he may prefer to exhibit a family coat of arms, a religious symbol, or a representation of a famous, heroic event.

The strength of a tapestry is in its weaves, the places where the threads intersect. The weaver strives to keep his weaves tight and straight so the fabric will maintain its resiliency.

For the two of us, a tapestry with its many innumerable weaves illustrates the idea of full-life generosity. Each weave represents one of the ways followers of Jesus express a life of giving rather than taking. Considered together, the weaves sum up the character and conduct of a fully developed Christ-follower.

We think there are seven such weaves, and we would like to introduce each of them to you in this final week of BeScrooged. As you reflect on each of them, think of the beautiful tapestry of full-life generosity that begins to emerge as we continue our daily drive up the seven rungs of the ladder to where we see Christ more and more as the center point of our lives.

The Seven Weaves of Full-Life Generosity

- A full-life generous person is a well-spring of cheer and kindness in his dealings with others. We call this the weave of being an encourager. Think about adding value to the lives of people you are meeting each day through words of affirmation, appreciation, and wisdom.
- A full-life generous person welcomes people into their private world, where they are accepted and befriended in the name of Jesus. We call this the weave of being hospitable. Think about those who are lonely—the neighbor, the newcomer, the seeker of faith—and crave the gift of friendship.
- A full-life generous person offers his time, energy, and skills to do things that someone cannot do by themselves. We call this the weave of being a servant. Think about the elderly, the poor, the person with special needs, the victim, and the young who need assistance to accomplish things they cannot do by themselves.
- A full-life generous person acts mercifully and restoratively toward our created world and the fragile lives that are broken around us (morally, physically, eco-

The 7 + 3 Weaves of Full-Life Generosity

TIGHTEN THE KNOTS OF THE WEAVE WITH

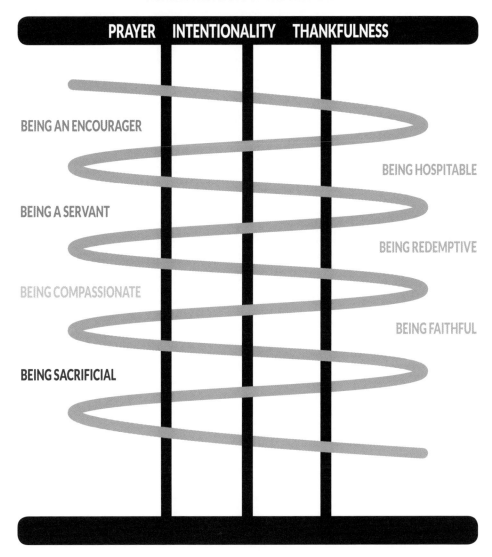

PRAYER   INTENTIONALITY   THANKFULNESS

BEING AN ENCOURAGER

BEING HOSPITABLE

BEING A SERVANT

BEING REDEMPTIVE

BEING COMPASSIONATE

BEING FAITHFUL

BEING SACRIFICIAL

nomically, environmentally). We call this the weave of being redemptive. Think about the person who has failed, who has made poor choices, and has been ostracized. Who will offer them grace, hope, and a fresh "welcome back" into a community of friends? Think about the marvelous creation God has made and gave us to steward and how we can seek better ways to respect and manage it better.

- A full-life generous person engages with those who are suffering (destitute, homeless, addicted, hungry) or who have been denied justice in the world. We call this the weave of being compassionate. Think about the most vulnerable— these could be immigrants, refugees, victims of war, the underprivileged, hungry children, and the homeless.
- A full-life generous person commits himself to a collection of Christ-following brothers and sisters who work hard to love one another and who, together, seek to make a difference in the lives of others. We call this the weave of being faithful. Think about people who band together to worship, to grow spiritually, to serve, and to support one another in times of difficulty.
- A full-life generous person believes the stewardship of their resources, which come from God, is a significant expression of their growing faith and journey. Therefore, they consider with great care what it means to give joyfully, purposefully, and thoughtfully. We call this the weave of being sacrificial. Think of worthy organizations—your church, faith-based ministries, schools—and unusually faithful people who are touching people with Jesus's gospel. Which ones seize the attention of your heart? Which ones will use your gifts wisely and effectively?

Tightening the Knots of the Weaves

When we set out to create a tapestry of full-life generosity, there are three constant efforts which are necessary.

Prayer: Our continuous conversation with God. This is our regular effort to commune with our Heavenly Father, speaking from our hearts and listening for whatever word he may impart to us. Our prayers are best kept simple, humble, and expectant. When we address God with simplicity, we use ordinary language that best expresses the urgent matters that live in our hearts. Humility emerges in our prayers when we speak to the Lord honestly, confessing our doubts, our fears, and our experience of brokenness and failure. We pray expectantly when we pray with faith, believing that God hears and responds to the most childlike of prayers and gives us direction and confidence.

Intentionality: We believe God has a purpose for each one of us. He prepares us for various forms of serving and giving. He calls us and generates passion and vision in our hearts. He empowers us to carry out his bidding.

Thankfulness: The Holy Scriptures are full of encouragements for us to be thankful people. To be thankful is to acknowledge that there are things that God does for us that we cannot do for ourselves.

To be thankful is to reflect on the value of what has been done for us each day.

To be thankful is to make sure that the generosity of God in our lives is never taken for granted.

As you read through the final part of Ebenezer Scrooge's story, watch how this once-mean old man begins to change. And when the story ends, make sure you see how so many of the weaves of full-life generosity have become center points of his new life.

WEEK FOUR

WE THINK THE BEGINNING OF WEEK IV IS AN APPROPRIATE PLACE to pause and to humbly acknowledge that *full-life* generosity represents a high standard for a life of giving that everyone, beginning with us, will struggle to attain.

We (Mark and Gordon) must express our repentance that, while we have strong convictions concerning *full-life* generosity, we have not always been faithful to those convictions. Every person, at every age, and place on the ladder needs BeScroogement. It starts with a commitment each morning as we get out of bed and put our feet on the ground and decide, "what sort of generous vessel can I be today?"

So, we are dedicated learners in this spiritual formation process, and we pray that God will give us fresh breakthroughs (BeScroogements) in the cultivation of the generous way. More than anything else, we want our families, our friends, and our brothers and sisters in the Christian movement to see us as men who are trying to "practice what we preach."

"When the Christmas morning service ended, I greeted as many people as I could. I gave coins to the children, invited the homeless to come and visit me, and offered a job to a young woman who was seeking employment. I made sure I spoke to the pastor to tell him how much his Christmas sermon had meant to an old man like me."

Christmas Day: BeScrooged

When I awoke that Christmas morning, I was—for a moment—completely disoriented. And why not? I'd spent a large part of the night "traveling" across city and countryside looking at my past, present, and future. Where was I now? And what day, what time, was it?

I looked about, seeking familiar things. Was this my pillow? My bed? My room? Three times I was able to say yes.

That meant I was still among the living, not buried in that miserable, neglected churchyard. It meant I must have been BeScrooged and offered an opportunity to transform my life. It also meant I'd be able to make amends to all those I'd hurt so badly in the past, that I could attempt to make a positive difference in the lives of people who were more unfortunate than I.

I don't have any time to waste, I thought. I have a lot to make up for.

"I'm dizzy with joy," I half-sang to myself as I crawled from my bed. "I feel as if I've drunk a bit more than I should have. I want to shout *Merry Christmas* to everyone in the world. And why not a Happy New Year too?" Isn't that what my nephew, Fred, did every Christmas Eve when he came to my office?

I began to convulse with laughter, and for a while I couldn't stop. It caused me to wonder how long it had been since I'd laughed at anything.

Then, in the distance, I heard the swell of church bells, followed by the shouts of happy people out on the streets.

Opening my bedroom window, I looked out. There at the corner was a boy dressed for church. I called out to him: "What's today?"

"Today? Why, it's Christmas Day," he answered. I could tell he was shocked that someone wouldn't know it was Christmas.

"I've not missed it," I said to myself. "Christmas is just beginning."

I asked the boy, "Do you know the meat store down the block where there's a huge turkey hanging on display?"

When he assured me that he did, I offered him money if he would go and purchase it for me. I said that I'd like to have it delivered to a family to whom I was in great debt. There would be a bonus for him, I said, if he hurried.

"I'll send the turkey to Bob Cratchit's home," I thought. "I'll send it anonymously. No one will ever know where it came from. Why that turkey is bigger than Tiny Tim!"

Quickly I shaved and dressed, went downstairs and joined the growing crowds in the streets. I gave a Merry Christmas greeting to everyone I met. I shook hands, gave hugs, and kissed a few elderly ladies.

Then I saw, coming toward me, the two gentlemen who had been in my office on Christmas Eve trying to solicit a donation for the poor.

"Hello there … hello!" I called out. "I hope your efforts were successful yesterday. A very Merry Christmas to you both."

"Mr. Scrooge?" one of them said, clearly astonished at my sudden friendliness.

"Yes. That's my name," I said. "I can't imagine that you find it a rather pleasant name after the way I treated you yesterday. Can I tell you how sorry I am … for the things I said to you?"

Neither of them knew what to say, so I spoke again.

"I have something to ask you," I continued. "If it isn't too late, I'd like to make a donation to your Christmas fund." Then I leaned in toward them so no one else would hear, and I whispered an amount of money so large that they gasped.

"Why….why …you …you can't be serious! Surely, you're fooling with us," one of the men said, as the size of my gift began to dawn on him.

"I've never been more serious, and I'm not making fun of you. The amount takes into account gifts I should have given in past years. I'll have a check waiting for you at my office tomorrow morning. Use it as you think best. I'm sure you'll be able to touch a lot of lives."

Something deep within me said, "Scrooge, you were made to do things like this."

I hurried on to our neighborhood church. When the Christmas morning service ended, I greeted as many people as I could. I gave coins to the children, invited the homeless to come and visit me, and offered a job to a young woman who was seeking employment. I made sure I spoke to the pastor to tell him how much his Christmas sermon had meant to an old man like me. He too seemed in shock when I left him at the altar.

I exited the church thinking that it really doesn't take a lot to lift and encourage people. You just have to get your mind off yourself for a while. How had I missed the joy that comes when you open your life and resources to others? Why, I wondered, had BeScroogement taken so long?

That afternoon, I headed for the home of my nephew, Fred, and his family. When they answered my knock and found me standing there, they didn't know what to say. But when they'd regained their senses, they pulled me through the door with embraces and kisses.

My, what an afternoon and evening we had together! There was food to eat, games to play, songs to sing. And the children! What can I say about those darling children? How can I describe their laughter, their affection, their innocence? They were so young, and fortunately for me, they had no idea of the kind of man I'd been. They just accepted me as I was that afternoon: BeScrooged and full of joy.

Again and again I found myself wiping away tears of delight. No one there could have appreciated what it meant to me that, for the first time in all my adult life, I belonged to a family.

Then Christmas Day was over. Reluctantly, I left Fred's lovely home and headed for my own home to prepare for the next day and the work that waited for me.

I'm sure more than a few people wondered what Ebenezer Scrooge would be like when he reached the offices of Scrooge and Marley the next morning. Had my Christmas Day conduct been some sort of temporary insanity that would dissipate the next morning when I smelled the money again? On December 26th, would I revert to being the same old Scrooge who did nothing but make life miserable for people? Would the effects of BeScroogement last?

I guess I was the only one who knew the answer to that question.

Arriving early at the office the next morning, I went straight to my desk. I wanted to be there when Bob Cratchit arrived.

If you're a micro-managing clock-watcher like I used to be, then you'd notice that Bob was six minutes and twenty seconds late. I watched him slip through the front door and tiptoe toward his desk, hoping I wouldn't notice him or what time it was.

I must admit that the old Ebenezer Scrooge would have been out of his mind with anger at Bob for being late.

But not the new BeScrooged man. He was ready for a little fun.

I shouted out in the voice of the old Scrooge, "Cratchit, what do you mean by coming to work late?"

Cratchit froze at the sound of my voice.

"I'm very sorry, sir," he said. "I know I'm late."

"You certainly are!" I grumbled. "Yes. Absolutely no doubt about it. Get in here!" I motioned for Cratchit to approach my desk.

"It's only once a year, sir," Bob pleaded as he came toward me. "It won't happen again. I'm afraid I had too good a time with my family yesterday. I drank a bit more wine than was prudent. And someone gave us an enormous turkey—"

"Now listen to me," I yelled at Bob. "I am not going to stand for this sort of conduct any longer." I leaped out of my chair and spoke as loudly as I could, "I am going to raise your salary!"

There was a moment of silence while we both just looked at each other.

The expression on Bob Cratchit's face defied description. You could almost see the wheels in his head turning. Had the old guy finally lost his mind, he must have wondered? He began to reach out very slowly for a wooden cane leaning against the wall. He must have been preparing to protect himself if I attacked him.

I could hold it in no longer. A smile began to spill across my face.

"Merry Day-After Christmas, Bob," I said gently, breaking the momentary silence. "I'm so glad you had a wonderful time with your family yesterday."

Saying this, I stepped forward and embraced my clerk. "This is going to be the best Christmas I've ever experienced in all my years. I'm not only going to raise your salary, I'm going to provide for Tiny Tim's medical bills. I'm going to assure that your family is well taken care of. We can talk about all of this and more when we have lunch together. Now, why don't you get a fire going in the stove. Use all the coal you want, and by the way, order more of it so we can warm up this place for once."

For me this moment with Bob Cratchit was unforgettable. To this day I think about what it must have been like for Bob to hear such powerful words of hope coming from a man like me. What he must have felt as he slowly came to realize that his boss, Ebenezer Scrooge, was a transformed man. A man no longer captive to a golden idol.

BeScroogement had done its work. Generosity was my new way of life.

DAY 22:
BEING AN ENCOURAGER

SOMETHING GENEROUS HAPPENS WHEN WE CHOOSE TO BE A WELLSPRING OF CHEER AND KINDNESS IN OUR DEALINGS WITH OTHERS. WE CALL THIS BEING AN ENCOURAGER.

"May the Lord show mercy to the house of Onesiphorus." (II Timothy 1:16-18)

HERE AND THERE IN THE PAGES OF SCRIPTURE ARE VIBRANT PEOPLE who have the ability to inject joy and hope into the human experience. They are the encouragers. Simply put: they press courage into others.

Significantly, God is an encourager. "I shall be with you," God says to Moses. "Today I have made you a fortified city," he reminds Jeremiah. "You are my son, and I am pleased with you," he declares to his son, Jesus. "Don't be afraid; keep on speaking, do not be silent," he whispers to Paul in Corinth.

Then, there is Onesiphorus. Ever hear of him? Most of us can hardly spell his name. Writing to one of his sons in the faith from prison, Paul says of Onesiphorus, "He often refreshed me." Paul adds, "[Onesiphorus] was not ashamed [that I was in jail]."

Others might have been fearful that, if they connected with Paul, they would be arrested also, and charged as co-conspirators. But Onesiphorus seems not to have been disturbed by this possibility. Paul needed encouragement, and Onesiphorus was determined to provide him with what he needed.

Paul also says of Onesiphorus, "When he was in Rome, he searched hard for me." Remember this single-mindedness when you imagine a huge, ancient city without phones or e-mail. How hard do you think it would have been to locate Paul? Many of us might have been tempted to give up the search in a short period of time. Not Onesiphorus.

Paul adds one final thing to Onesiphorus' resume as an encourager: "You know how very well and in how many ways he helped me at Ephesus."

Quite a man, this encourager-friend of Paul's. He had the ability to be loyal, to provide cheer, and do deeds of kindness. He knew the right things to say, the appropriate things to do. When he was around, people who were down, feeling defeated, or uncertain of the future were elevated. That's why Paul wrote of being warmed and strengthened in spirit when Onesiphorus came to see him. Fear, doubt, and gloom drift away when you have a friend like this who can make you feel loved, appreciated, and worthy.

There are others in Paul's world like Onesiphorus. Take Stephanas, Fortunatus, and Achaius. Again, strange names. Of these men Paul said, "They refreshed my spirit." Then there's Titus: "God comforted us by his coming." And don't forget Paul's comment about the mother of Rufus: "[She] has been a mother to me." One has the sense that she understood the value of a warm blanket, chicken soup, and (please, God) chocolate chip cookies.

People like these seem to know how to speak into dark moods and dispositions every time they connect with people. Something—you could call it a spiritual power—flows from their hearts, and it affects others for the good. When encouragers are in motion, you pick up something of what the kindness of Jesus must have been like.

Back to Onesiphorus. He offers us a glimpse of the first step in full-life generous living. He helps us see that the way we greet people, the way we affirm them, and the way we express appreciation for things they've done all make an enormous difference. Or, take the way we uphold those who are in need of a motivating word, the way we speak softly, graciously, to those who are sad or low, the way we give a gesture of blessing, a prayer for strength: these also can be powerful growing experiences in generous living.

In the larger world, where there is more than enough violence and selfishness, the follower of Christ must project this kind of penetrating joy that lifts the heart and induces change in the moods of people. These life-giving experiences can take place on a bus, in traffic, in the work-place, in a restaurant, or in the market while we wait in line. In short, there is a call for full-life generous givers wherever there are people with hearts needing something that looks and sounds like love.

People who already live generously understand this.

Ebenezer asks: Do you know anyone who fits the description of an Onesiphorus? What is it about this person that causes you to think so highly of him or her? What qualities of character and personality do they possess that you would like to see in yourself?

Reflection: Complete this thought: One of the most memorable experiences of encouragement in my life happened when…

BeScrooged Activity: There are a number of ways we can seek to be encouragers. Here are a few ideas to get you started.

- Find a unique way to express appreciation to someone for something they have done. Be as creative as possible, so this person can see the time, thought, and effort you put into your message of gratitude.
- If you know someone who is under great stress, who is suffering, or who has sustained a great loss, what can you do to offer a word of care and concern?
- Make a small list of men and women who are in public leadership. Examples: school-teachers, law enforcement, fire service, and local government officials. Consider writing some of them notes of appreciation and encouragement.

DAY 23:
BEING HOSPITABLE

SOMETHING GENEROUS HAPPENS WHEN WE CHOOSE TO WELCOME PEOPLE INTO OUR PRIVATE WORLDS SO THEY CAN EXPERIENCE ACCEPTANCE AND FRIENDSHIP. WE CALL THIS BEING HOSPITABLE.

"The jailer brought them into his house and set a meal before them. He was filled with joy because he had come to believe in God—he and his whole family." (Acts 16:22-34)

THE SCRIPTURES WERE WRITTEN IN A TIME WHEN HOSPITALITY—the opening of one's home to the traveler, the stranger, the friend—was considered a core cultural value. The world was a dangerous place, especially after dark. The only safe places were inside someone's home or someone's tent.

It was universally understood that a guest in one's home was to be treated with honor. He was to be fed, given a place to rest, and guaranteed protection. Hospitality was among the most noble of gestures in ancient times. It was a mark of the Christian way to offer hospitality not only to one's friends and countrymen, but even to the alien.

Several exceptional examples of hospitality occur in the New Testament. Elizabeth and Zechariah received a pregnant Mary, soon-to-be mother of our Lord, into their home for several months. Mary, Martha, and their brother Lazarus often hosted Jesus and his disciples in their home and offered them food and relaxation. Aquila and Priscilla invited Apollos into their home so he could be further mentored in the ways of the gospel of Christ. Then there are Paul's words to Philemon, "Prepare a guest room for me because I hope to be restored to you in answer to your prayers." (Philemon 1:22)

A favorite of many is the story of the Philippian jailer who "entertained" Paul and

Silas in the darkest part of his prison one night, locking their feet in stocks. Let's agree that, for Paul and Silas, the evening did not start with a surge of hospitality.

Then around midnight—while Paul and Silas were praying and singing rather than complaining—a strong earthquake hit the area. The violent tremor created a role reversal. The jailer, terrified that he'd lost his prisoners, prepared to take his own life. In that moment Paul and Silas, now liberated from captivity, took charge. They assured the jailer that he need not hurt himself and shared the redeeming story of Jesus. Soon, the jailer, his wife, and the rest of his household declared their desire to become Christ-followers.

The result? Hospitality. "At that hour of the night the jailer took them and washed their wounds; then immediately he and all his family were baptized. The jailer brought them into his house and set a meal before them; [the jailer] was filled with joy because he had come to believe in God—he and his whole family." (Acts 16:33) One could say hospitality was the first sign that a man and his family had been genuinely converted to Christian faith.

For most of us, our home is the most private place in our lives. We send an important message when we open the door and invite others in to spend an hour with us, when we welcome them to our table to eat and drink with us, or when we offer them a place to stay. If, however, we live in an urban environment where entertainment space is limited, we may have to use restaurant space or other public places to show hospitality to others.

But hospitality is more than this. It can involve a revealing of the deeper spaces in our lives to those who might profit from knowing a bit of the story of how we came to follow Jesus. It can be our willingness to share what God has taught us in the hard moments of life. Hospitality also happens when we open our lives to younger people who need the wisdom and direction of someone who has had many more years to learn God's ways. Hospitality is helping people get away from difficult and stressful situations and offering them a moment of quiet and rest.

Hospitality is not the exclusive offering of the rich. It can happen in the simplest of places with the smallest of gifts. The key to hospitality lies not in lavish entertainment, but in the warmth and openness with which we give of ourselves.

People who live generously believe in hospitality and carefully consider those times when the front door—not just of one's home but also of one's heart—needs to be opened. The Philippian jailer took Paul and Silas into his home, not out to eat.

Ebenezer asks: Think of a time when you experienced the ultimate in hospitality from someone you loved and admired. What made that such a special occasion? Can you recall a time when you were the giver of hospitality? What effect did it have on you?

Reflection: Why is hospitality sometimes a difficult challenge for us?

BeScrooged Activity: There is a broad range of ways to be hospitable to others. Here are some ideas to get you started:

- Extend yourself to assist people who are struggling: the elderly, the disabled, young mothers with children, strangers who are lost. What courtesies can you offer in a brief encounter?
- Invite someone to breakfast or lunch and make sure you direct the conversation to things that are important to them. This is a time when it's not about you.
- Invite a small group of people from your neighborhood or church to your home or apartment. Try to choose people who do not know each other very well. Ask each person to tell the group something about his or her life story. *How did (s)he get here?*
- In many parts of this world there is a prevailing spirit of rudeness and spitefulness. What can you do to properly engage a stranger with a smile, a greeting, or appropriate conversation that demonstrates you care?

DAY 24:
BEING A SERVANT

SOMETHING GENEROUS HAPPENS WHEN WE CHOOSE TO OFFER OUR TIME AND SKILL AND JOIN OTHERS IN THE "DOING OF THINGS" THAT CANNOT BE DONE ALONE. WE CALL THIS BEING A SERVANT.

"Now that I, your Lord and Teacher, have washed your feet, you also should wash one another's feet. I have set you an example that you should do as I have done for you."
(John 13:14-15)

WHEN OUR LORD SELECTED HIS DISCIPLES, most of them considered it an opportunity to rise to influential positions in the world of organized religion. Of course they were drawn to his brand of teaching, but they may have been even more attracted to the possibility of his ascending the religious hierarchy at Jerusalem's temple.

You can imagine their private dreams and conversations. Who would be in charge of this or that? How much wealth might they accumulate? And, if there came a day when Jesus relinquished his position or something happened to him, which of them might be in a position to become his successor?

So it must have been something of a surprise when it dawned on them that this was not Jesus's perspective. Following him and embracing his gospel was not an invitation to religious royalty; rather, it was an opportunity to live like a servant.

At no point was this lesson brought home more dramatically than on the night when the disciples joined the Lord to eat the annual Passover meal, a Passover meal that would turn out to be his last. There came a moment while they were all eating when Jesus shed his outer clothing, wrapped a towel about his waist, took a bowl of water, and began to wash his disciples' feet.

Now, this washing of feet was not a ceremonial exercise as it is today in some Christian traditions. It was a necessary task that should have been done long before the moment Jesus began to do it.

Filthy feet caked with mud that contained disease, animal and human waste, and garbage thrown from the front doors of homes. Feet infected with sores and scabs. Feet whose smell goes far beyond the wildest imagination.

Furthermore, in ancient thinking the soles of one's feet were presumed to attract the sins of the earth. So, to touch people's feet and wash them was simply unthinkable! No act was more humble, more menial.

Yet the Son of God did just this! One wonders why none of the other disciples had thought to take on this odious responsibility. The fact is that none did.

Simon Peter's spirited objection to Jesus's actions is evidence of how shocked everyone must have been. Simon only quieted down when he was firmly rebuked by the Lord.

At the end of this foot-washing, Jesus said, "Do you understand what I have done?… Now that I, your Lord and teacher, have washed your feet, you should also wash one another's feet." (John 13:12)

This was Jesus's way of dramatizing the great unifying act of following Christ: *We serve each other. We do the humblest things out of love and regard for each other. We emulate the Savior not as kings, but as servants. And having served one another, we go out into the larger world to live a life of serving as well.*

Living as a servant is about cultivating a keen eye for those around us who are weak, disabled, or struggling, and coming to their side to do with them and for them what they cannot—at the moment—do for themselves.

But the idea of servanthood is even greater than this. To serve one another is to create an environment in which those around us can be helped in practical ways but are also encouraged to grow to the fullness of whatever it is God wants them to be. We ignore this principle to our peril.

Implications: A husband serves his wife as she serves him. Parents serve their children. Friends serve friends. Christ-followers serve their associates in the marketplace, their neighbors, even the stranger. This idea of full-life generous living can become quite radical if one allows it to be. That's what frightened Simon Peter. And that's why Jesus made such an issue of it all.

Ebenezer asks: Who do you know that understands and practices the dynamic of servanthood exchanges? What made you select this person as an example? Are there issues in your life that make serving others difficult, or do you find this to be a natural inclination in your personal relationships?

Reflection: Complete this thought: What discourages me from being more of a servant is… What encourages me to be more of a servant is…

BeScrooged Activity: Start at home, in your neighborhood or your apartment complex, and begin finding simple ways that you can be a servant to your spouse, roommate, or those who are around you. How can you "go the extra mile" to serve them? Can you clean, sweep, do the dishes, take out the trash? Do something that stretches you and that really helps someone else.

DAY 25:
BEING REDEMPTIVE

SOMETHING GENEROUS HAPPENS WHEN WE CHOOSE TO ACT MERCIFULLY AND RESTORATIVELY TOWARD THOSE WHOSE LIVES ARE BROKEN. WE CALL THIS BEING REDEMPTIVE.

"Jesus said, 'Simon.....do you truly love me more than these?' 'Yes, Lord, you know that I love you.' Jesus said, 'Feed my lambs.'" (John 21:15)

THE PROPHET MICAH OFFERS ONE OF THE MOST IMPORTANT INSIGHTS concerning the nature of the God of the Bible. "Who is a God like you," Micah asks, "who pardons sin and forgives the transgressions of the remnant of his inheritance? For you do not stay angry forever but delight to show mercy. You will again have compassion on us; you will tread our sins underfoot and hurl our iniquities into the depths of the sea." (Micah 7:18)

Most ancient people knew only of gods who were consistently angry, demanding, and punitive. The consequence? People lived in fear of the unexpected and the unknown.

Not so, Micah says, with the God of the Bible. A most important aspect of God's character is mercy. He never turns his back upon the repentant, the truly sorrowful sinner. This is redemption.

Generous living reflects this aspect of God. It renounces accusation and judgment. It does not walk in the way of gloating, vindictiveness, shunning. There is, in the heart of one who lives generously, the gracious instinct to forgive and restore.

"If someone is caught in a sin, you who are spiritual should restore him gently," (Galatians 6:1) St. Paul wrote. Strange words from a man who had formerly lived a life of violence and persecution. But as a follower of Christ, he was now one who lived generously. Having known forgiveness and restoration in his own life, he understood that at the spear-point of the gospel of Jesus there was an urgency to receive broken people in a spirit of mercy and grace.

Perhaps one of the most dramatic illustrations of redemption came in the life of Simon Peter, who, having claimed an undying loyalty to Jesus, a few hours later vehemently denied he had ever known him. Think about this: Peter actually swore—after having followed Jesus for three years—that he'd never seen him before in his life.

The Lord had warned him that something like this was going to happen, but Peter didn't listen.

Some days after that terrible night, the two met in the early morning hours at a campfire on the shore of Lake Galilee. Jesus's intention? To extend to Simon a most remarkable gift of mercy. That morning over breakfast, the earlier episode of betrayal was "trodden underfoot," to use Micah's words. The Lord restored Peter to his place as friend and disciple and to his call to be a leader in the Christian movement.

Jesus's merciful gesture was full-life generosity in action. And Peter clearly never forgot it.

What happened that morning—that generous act of redemption—presents us with this question. How generous are we when it comes to extending the hand of forgiveness and redemption to those who have failed in life—or perhaps, have failed us?

If we insist on holding grudges, never forgetting, seeking our own versions of revenge upon those who have hurt or betrayed us, there can be no growth in the generous spirit. If we fail to seek out the one who strayed from the fellowship, then our quest to be people of generosity begins to dissipate.

Forgiveness, restoration, the gift of a second chance: these are the pathways to the blessedness of full-life generous living.

Ebenezer asks: Can you think of a time when you saw someone who had hit life's bottom and was treated with disdain and severe judgment? What happened to that person? Conversely, do you know of anyone who has been showered with the redeeming grace of others? Forgiven? Restored? Welcomed back?

Reflection: Who are the people in our world who might feel the most unwelcome in our churches? What might we say to them? What can we do for them?

BeScrooged Activity: Are you aware of someone who has gone through an experience of failure or disgrace? Could this be a time to write that person a letter of encouragement, an assurance of prayer? Could this be a time to inquire of people in leadership if there should be some sort of restorative effort? (Please note: this is a very important initiative, but one should not pursue these actions without the wisdom of someone who knows the situation well and is able to advise an appropriate response.)

DAY 26:
BEING COMPASSIONATE

SOMETHING GENEROUS HAPPENS WHEN WE CHOOSE TO BECOME INVOLVED WITH THOSE WHO ARE SUFFERING, OR WHEN WE STAND WITH THOSE WHO HAVE BEEN DENIED JUSTICE IN THE WORLD. WE CALL THIS BEING COMPASSIONATE.

"When Jesus landed and saw a large crowd, he had compassion on them because they were like sheep without a shepherd." (Mark 6:34)

COMPASSION, MEANING CO-SUFFERING, is one of the Bible's most significant words. In the early pages of the Old Testament, we learn of a God who is not unaware that his people are suffering. "I have indeed seen the misery of my people in Egypt...I have heard the crying out because of their slave drivers...I have come down to rescue them from the hand of the Egyptians..." (Excerpts from Exodus 3:7-8)

If this is the true nature of God—and this is a very, very big idea—then it behooves those who are his people to make sure they are attuned to the same signals: the cry of the suffering, the anguish of the oppressed, the anger of the mistreated.

So, Moses stands before the Egyptian pharaoh and strenuously pleads his case for the Hebrews who live in slavery. Daniel insists that the Babylonian king "renounce [his] sins by doing what is right, and [his] wickedness by being kind to the oppressed." (Daniel 4:27)

Esther, at the risk of her own life, approaches her husband, the king, and calls his attention to the possibility that the Hebrew people (her people) will be slaughtered if certain members of his administration have their way. Nathan confronts David and forces him to face up to what he has done by committing adultery with Bathsheba and arranging for the death of her husband.

In each of these cases, someone has done what the victims could not have done for themselves.

It is worrisome that many good people who believe their lives to be grounded on the scriptures have a stunted understanding of justice. They do not perceive that our God could be displeased when his people feel no sensitivity or responsibility for those places in the world (often beginning right beyond the church door) where people are denied opportunities and protections that others enjoy.

Jesus was particularly animated when he confronted the Pharisees. He saw people who were experts when it came to traditional religious procedures, but who had no empathy whatsoever for those about them who were in great distress and had no one to speak up for their cause. "You give God a tenth," Jesus said, "but you neglect justice and the love of God." (Luke 11:42)

One who lives generously prays for a prophetic eye that he might see those who are powerless or voiceless, those who are unable to speak or act for themselves. And when prompted by the Holy Spirit, he is prepared to speak up in their place with the same kind of bravery Jesus had.

The word that best describes this perspective is *compassion*. It means that *one's heart becomes so aligned with those who are deprived that there is a sharing of the pain and an urgency to do whatever can be done to alleviate it.*

"I have compassion for these people," (Mark 8:2) Jesus says of several thousand people who had not eaten for three days. Nothing will satisfy him until the disciples have begun an effort to feed them.

Compassion may begin with a proactive sensitivity, but it translates into appropriate action. Compassion's effort ends only when suffering is diminished. No one demonstrated this better than our Savior. His compassion led to people being fed.

Ebenezer asks: Is there a group of suffering people in this world that draws your attention more than any other group? Why do you think God has caused you to notice this group?

Reflection: What can block a person from being compassionate?

BeScrooged Activity: There are people who cross our path every day whose lives are shattered for a myriad of reasons. Ask God to sensitize you to one of them. What physical gift (not money or food) might you give that would lighten the load of this person? Present it to them directly and include a letter of encouragement and support.

DAY 27:
BEING FAITHFUL

SOMETHING GENEROUS HAPPENS WHEN WE CHOOSE TO PARTICIPATE SELFLESSLY AND COOPERATIVELY IN A COMMUNITY OF BROTHERS AND SISTERS GIVEN TO US BY GOD. THE BIBLE ACTUALLY CALLS THIS LAYING DOWN OUR LIVES FOR ONE ANOTHER. WE CALL IT BEING FAITHFUL.

"Let us draw near to God with a sincere heart...Let us hold unswervingly to the hope we profess...Let us consider how we may spur one another on toward love and good deeds... Let us not give up meeting together as some are in the habit of doing...Let us encourage one another—and all the more as you see the Day approaching."
(Hebrews 10:21-25)

"Out of the most severe trial their overflowing joy and extreme poverty welled up in rich generosity." (II Corinthians 8:2)

THE LARGE NEW TESTAMENT BOOK CALLED HEBREWS was written to Christians who were experiencing severe persecution. They appear to have been a people who were lacking in courage and the ability to mutually support one another. Some Christians were renouncing their faith. More than a few leaders had succumbed to fear and had given up their responsibilities, some even their faith.

Bottom line: the book of Hebrews is for people who are temporarily stumbling, who seem to have forgotten what the "Christian way" is all about.

The writer—often thought to be Paul—wrote this book in order to elevate the courage of the people and their spiritual leaders. He acknowledged that times were tough.

But faithful Christians hold on, he wrote, and they band tightly together for the purposes of giving and finding strength in one another.

One of the most important things a full-life generous Christ-follower gives is himself. He commits to a gathering of people that we call the church. He doesn't expect this church to be full of perfect people. He knows there will be letdowns, failures, and periods of spiritual aridity. He understands there will be disagreements and misunderstandings. Perhaps there will be times when the routines of local church life seem boring and impractical.

But if there are full-life generous people who will give themselves to this venture called church, amazing things can happen as they are unleashed into their personal worlds.

The writer of Hebrews challenges his readers with these brief, bulleted statements: "Let us draw near to God"..."let us hold on to the hope [of the gospel of Christ]"..."let us spur each other on toward love and good deeds"..."let's not give up meeting together"..."let us encourage one another." These statements serve an important function, especially for people living in a time when stress is high and there is a need for wisdom and power. In short, the writer is saying, you guys desperately need each other.

Referring to one gathering where people did these kinds of things, Paul wrote, "Out of the most severe trial their overflowing joy and extreme poverty welled up in rich generosity." (II Corinthians 8:2)

How can this be? How can a ragtag collection of baby Christ-followers be spoken of in such exquisite terms? Answer: When people are enthusiastically generous (full-life generous), there is a beauty to their community that no one else can replicate.

Ebenezer asks: If you are part of a fellowship of people (called a church), how do you imagine that you are perceived? As faithful? As contributing? Caring? Generous? Or are you seen as one who is aloof and distant? Undependable? Uninvolved?

Reflection: What do you desire in a church experience? To be entertained? Or to be a part of a gathering of people who wish, through full-life generosity, to change a bit of their world in the name of Jesus? Ask yourself this important question: what strengths do I have that could make a difference in the life of my church?

BeScrooged Activity: Invite a group of friends and acquaintances to your home for an evening. Introduce these sentences one at a time as thought-provokers that might encourage an evening of conversation.
1.   What does it mean to you to be a generous Christian?
2.   After reviewing the four challenges that the Hebrews writer offers, which one do you think your church needs to practice most?
3.   What does it mean to encourage one another? How would you like to be encouraged?
4.   Who do you know that spurs others on to love and good work? What is he or she like?
5.   How can we help each other hold fast to the hope in a challenging world?

DAY 28:
BEING SACRIFICIAL

SOMETHING GENEROUS HAPPENS WHEN WE CHOOSE TO BE A GOOD STEWARD OF WHAT WE HAVE AND GIVE PURPOSEFULLY, JOYFULLY, AND SACRIFICIALLY FROM THE RESOURCES GOD HAS PROVIDED US. WE CALL THIS BEING SACRIFICIAL.

"All the believers were one in heart and mind. No one claimed that any of his possessions was his own, but they shared everything they had." (Acts 4:32)

WE SHOULD NOT FAIL TO RECOGNIZE THAT THE FIRST GREAT EVENT in the life of the early church had to do with money. Money that was given joyfully, strategically, and sacrificially. Almost recklessly.

Something must have stirred people's hearts when they responded to the gospel of the love of Christ. It is interesting that we cannot find anyone who organized the giving of Christ-followers, or who went out and raised funds among the richest members of the community. This first giving event was not built on pleading with people or manipulating them. It was instigated by their fresh understanding of Jesus's message and the fact that they were part of a new community. Those newly converted to Jesus looked around, saw human need, felt compelled to give to it, and were blessed by the experience of seeing Jesus's full-life generosity vision and message more clearly.

In the past most of these people had lived under a religious system where giving was carefully regulated and probably corrupted. But now they felt free to provide for one another and to experience the genuine joy that occurs when resources move from hand to hand and make a difference in people's lives.

Not every collection of Christ-followers became this enthusiastic. The Corinthians—arguably the most prosperous of the early churches—seemed reluctant to give, while the Thessalonians—perhaps the poorest of the early churches—could not give enough. The difference between the two? Hard to say. Probably it had something to do with leadership or the way people perceived and applied the Christian gospel.

The writers God used to author the scriptures seem uniform in their recognition that giving out of one's personal treasure makes all the difference in increasing the depth of one's faith. If a person engages in all possible religious expressions, accumulates vast stores of theological knowledge, and exhausts himself in participating in fine programs, but ignores the gift of giving from his personal storehouse, his life of faith will never reach maturity.

So we read in the Old Testament of Israel learning how to give. We hear the prophets making it clear that the spiritual vitality of the nation demands an obedient and enthusiastic generosity. We see Jesus urging the faithfulness of giving to some of the poorest people and calling it true generosity. And we read Paul's forceful teaching to the Corinthians, in which he says: "You know the grace of our Lord Jesus Christ, that though he was rich, yet for your sakes he became poor, so that you through his poverty might become rich." (II Corinthians 8:2)

Genuine faith in our Lord Jesus Christ must show itself in our personal economics.

The ultimate standard of this generosity is sacrifice. Sacrifice means a level of giving in which one denies himself objects, privileges, or experiences that are rightfully his. *A sacrificial giver gives until it hurts.*

Jesus was the consummate sacrificial giver. What more can one give than his life? As he said to his disciples, "The son of man did not come to be served, but to serve, and to give his life a ransom for many."

With some exceptions, most of us will never be asked to literally give our lives. But we will be asked—should we wish to grow as mature Christ-followers—to give sacrificially and experience God our Father, Jesus, and the power of the Holy Spirit more deeply. And when that happens, the full-life meaning of generosity will become more clear.

Ebenezer asks: If generosity is ultimately understood as giving which is cheerful, sacrificial, and wise, consider how these three qualities are present in your financial plan of giving.

Reflection: Once again ask yourself, what should be the limits on my choices to spend and acquire? Am I confident that God looks on my spending habits with approval?

BeScrooged Activity: Consider developing a five-year giving plan. Decide on a percentage of your income that you will budget toward full-life generosity activities. Could you increase that percentage each year?

A Final Word from Scrooge

So there you have it. My BeScroogement, the journey I made from being a mean, miserly old man to what some now call full-life generosity. For me this journey was not only about money but about every other aspect of the man I have become. Full-life generosity is just that: *full life.*

Each morning as I arise to a new day, there is a question that demands a fresh answer: *what can I be, what can I do, what can I give that will make a difference in someone else's life?* As far as I can see, that's the supreme question for anyone who desires to practice full-life generosity.

Today, I see people differently. I walk the streets of my neighborhood and try to engage everyone I meet with a word of cheer and encouragement. I laugh with the children, offer my arm to the elderly, and try whenever possible to assist the disabled along their way. I ask God to make me a dispenser of grace wherever I go.

When I am with members of my family or in the company of my very best friends, I try to be a listener, to ask questions, to applaud things that they have accomplished. And when they come my way for advice and wisdom, I thank them for coming and I try to speak gently into their hearts.

There are things in this world that have awakened my heart with compassion. I hear of far-off villages where young people are poorly educated, where sanitation is primitive and disease is rampant, where women are abused and young men are pressed into brutal military service. I read of places where the strong oppress the weak and poor, where justice simply does not exist … but should.

Sometimes I take trips to places in need of schools, medical clinics, and clean water. And on each occasion I say to God, "Lord, show me where I can play a role here." Is this a place for me to offer my expertise? A place that needs a bit of my wealth? A place that I should pray for and tell others about?

My home is sizable, comfortable. I love to welcome people through the same door where I once saw Jacob Marley's face. I often host evenings of food and enriching conversation. I'm always glad when I can provide an overnight stay for someone who has no other place to go. People have made commitments to Christ as Lord while in my home.

I often ask myself, who in the younger generation might profit from the friendship of an older, more experienced man like myself if I were available to them? Who in leadership in our community, in our church, or in our government needs the wisdom that comes through growing old as I have?

I work hard at being faithful to my church. I am not like everyone in the congregation. We are all different people of varying ages and tastes. But we are committed to each other. It can be a humbling arrangement, but it builds a stronger spirit in me every time we are together.

And, of course, generosity always forces the question of what I will do with my material wealth. Be it a small amount or large, it is still God's to command and mine to manage. To whom will I give it? What results might I expect? You must understand that I take very seriously the investments I make in the work of Jesus in our world.

These are some of the things I think about every day since those ghosts did their BeScrooging work on me. These are things I pray about, and these are things I talk about with others whom I trust. These are also the hopes and dreams I talk and think about for our world and I wonder what it would be like if we could all begin to embrace them as personal eternal truths. And we all agree when we have those conversations: it's a great, great privilege to live generously, full-life generosity.

Christ has no body but yours,
No hands, no feet on earth but yours,
Yours are the eyes with which he looks
Compassion on this world,
Yours are the feet with which he walks to do good,
Yours are the hands, yours are the feet,
Yours are the eyes, you are his body.

(Teresa of Ávila)

ABOUT THE AUTHORS

GORDON MACDONALD

Gordon MacDonald is a pastor, bestselling author, and a frequent speaker to church and business leaders. For more than a decade he has used his 50+ years of ministry to encourage leaders, pastors and churches to new vision that introduces a worldwide paradigm shift of Christian generosity. He believes this movement can redeem lives and introduce new ways that will encourage churches to embrace the generous ways of the 1st century Christian church.

Gordon has been chancellor of Denver Seminary since 2011. He has pastored congregations in New York City, southern Illinois, and Kansas, among other locations. Most recently he served more than two decades as senior minister at Grace Chapel in Lexington, Massachusetts. He also was president for three years of the energetic nationwide campus ministry InterVarsity Christian Fellowship.

Gordon has ministered to a mass international audience through his many writings and books dealing with the intersection of spiritual leadership, soul growth and the gift of generosity given to us by God. Among his best-known works, *Ordering Your Private World* (2007) has appeared in a dozen languages, with nearly 1.5 million copies in print, and was honored by the Evangelical Christian Publishing Association with its Gold Medallion and Platinum awards. MacDonald's other books include *Renewing Your Spiritual Passion* (1997), *Secrets of a Generous Life* (2002), *Mid-Course Correction* (2005), *A Resilient Life* (2006), and *Building Below the Waterline: Shoring Up the Foundations of Leadership* (2011). He is an editor-at-large and regular contributor to *Leadership Journal*, a publication of Christianity Today, Inc.

Until 2007, MacDonald was also chairman of the board of the World Relief Corporation, an evangelical Christian organization devoted to alleviating poverty and suffering around the world.

MacDonald and his wife of more than fifty years, Gail, take their greatest joy from their two adult children and five grandchildren. They also love to read, kayak, hike, and bike.

MARK MACDONALD

Mark MacDonald is a creative branding and viral marketing specialist whose highly effective campaigns have helped businesses, churches, and ministries shape a powerful message and share it with enormous and diverse audiences. Founder and president of the marketing and media consulting firm Canterbury Partners, MacDonald has leveraged the firm's specialized know-how to help build the Christian generosity and wealth stewardship movement, playing key roles in the development of innovative organizations such as Generous Giving, Kingdom Advisors, Generous Church, and Crown Financial Ministry's MoneyLife initiative.

Canterbury Partners' other clients have ranged from major corporations such as Federal Express, Gillette, IBM, Texaco, Staples and Unilever, to influential Christian ministries including Focus on the Family and Promise Keepers, to humanitarian organizations like World Relief and World Vision.

Mark was a consultant to Saddleback Church and then later became the president of The Purpose Driven Life (PDL) movement. He led and engineered a marketing strategy for the brand that helped propel pastor Rick Warren's *The Purpose Driven Life* (2002) to its perch as the top-selling hardcover nonfiction book in history, with more than 30+ million books sold. Mark helped to develop innovative sales channels to reach consumers in more than 30,000 churches, thousands of Starbucks coffee shops, the United States military, professional sports organizations from the NFL, PGA to the NBA, and 32 state and 15 federal prisons.

In addition Mark has held several leadership positions in marketing and management ministries, helping them communicate with a postmodern world through film and other creative media. During Mark's tenure the organization garnered special recognition from the New York Film Festival, Telly Awards, Mobius Awards, and American Advertising Awards.